Vermont Life Stories

Memories of Summer Living in the Green Mountain State.

By

Margaret Berger Morse

© 2001 by Margaret Berger Morse. All rights reserved.

No part of this book may be reproduced, stored in a retrieval system, or transmitted by any means, electronic, mechanical, photocopying, recording, or otherwise, without written permission from the author.

ISBN: 0-75966-426-9

This book is printed on acid free paper.

1stBooks - rev. 10/16/01

For My Sisters: Barbara, Jeanne and Bobbie

Thank You for the Wonderful Memories!

To All Vermont Enthusiasts

TABLE OF CONTENTS

FOREWARD

Summers in Vermont whether living life on the shores of Lake Champlain, and/or traveling through the mountains of Green Mountain National Forest, and/or the roads and byways of the Northeast Kingdom, and/or the grand islands of South and North Hero, and/or the many wonderful explorations of Southern Vermont are always filled with new adventure. One never knows what each day will bring.

This is true no matter where one dwells.

This little book contains tales from my perception of my family, memories of many fun-filled summers spent in Vermont, primarily in the Long Point, Lake Champlain area and Green Mountains.

For those who are Vermont 'lovers' you know that there is so much more. I have not touched on winter, the many places and adventures for the snow-oriented person.

* * *

PART I

A BRIEF HISTORY OF LONG POINT

Through the years summering in Vermont on Long Point I have heard various stories of its beginnings.

Originally known as Camp Meeting Point as far back as 1880/1890s, Long Point was owned by Artimus Ball who occupied a large farm that included this piece of land. Various locations on the point were leased to campers by a number of caretakers/guardians who were responsible for the farm.

Most campers in those early years set up tents to sleep and eat in. Often a small shack was set up for a cooking stove and where the meals were prepared. There was a storehouse for supplies and the necessary outhouse behind this building.

One of the earliest camps built was *Bristol Lodge* near the top of the point. Perhaps it was the first. After it burned down in 1996 the new owner of the leased property Tom Paine told me that he had found a few artifacts up in the rock ledges from earlier periods. One piece was an old high-heeled boot that he thought might be of the late 1800's vintage.

There were also two other small cottages where *Maple Lodge* and *the Tops* were located. These were probably the ones that the Ball family had built and according to Bertha Stillson Ranger, in her reminiscences of Long Point were used chiefly by newly weds.

In the late 1950's the Ball farm, after a long line of various family living there, was sold to The Long Point Realty Corporation. This group governed by a Board made up of property lease owners controls and regulates how things are done.

PART II

THE BERGER FAMILY - VERMONT EXPERIENCE

My Dad, the Rev. Robert Birdsey Berger and my Mom, Frances Backer Berger, first came to Long Point on the shore of Lake Champlain North Ferrisburgh, Vermont in the summer of 1936. My oldest sister, Barbara, was one year old. They came as guests of a seminarian friend of my Dad.

My Dad was a Presbyterian preacher in Kingston, New Jersey, a 1933 graduate of Princeton Seminary, Princeton University.

This friend had said to my Dad, "Come along if you like. I have been invited to that lake in Vermont. I have never been there, but I'm game." So my Mom, Dad, baby Barbara, and their friends went. My Dad loved it and thus began the Berger family trek to Vermont nearly every August for the next thirty-five years.

The seminarian friend never went back.

My parents stayed at *the Avalon* known somewhat later as *the Retreat* that first year and during the next several years rented camps on the North Road: *the Just A Mere, the Princeton, Maple Lodge,* and on the East Road: *the Middlebury, the Leo Lodge* and other unnamed camps. I have a picture of my Mom sitting on the rocks in front of *the Middlebury*. This was before I was born.

* * *

My first memory of Long Point begins around the time I was four, about 1947. My family was renting *This Is The Limit (the Limit)* out on the end of the point, at the bottom of the hill, east off North Road.

Every year except for the two summers of 1957 and 1958 when we went to Estes Park, Colorado, my family went to Vermont to spend the month of August. Our family always went to Vermont. It didn't matter in what part of the country we lived. We lived in New Jersey, Missouri, Illinois and Ohio during those years.

We usually stayed four weeks, though my sister Barbara tells me there were a few summers when we only went for two and once three weeks. She also suggested that there was a year when we did not go at all. This was during the years of World War II.

* * *

Our family always left for vacation on the last Sunday of July or the first one of August after the evening prayer service at my dad's church.

All the suitcases, one for each of us, six, were packed and ready to go in the car before the service. And there was one extra suitcase with sheets and towels.

My sisters and I did not have to go to the evening service. The four of us would be sitting, waiting in readiness for the drive ahead, and in anticipation for the adventures to come on our vacation in Vermont.

Dad and Mom would arrive home from church and change clothes. Dad would pack the trunk with all the suitcases and any other baggage such as his fishing poles and gear, boxes of food, etc. He had a knack for packing because he always got everything in the trunk of the Buick. Dad always drove a Buick.

There was always a box in the front of the car by our Mom that had a picnic in it for the trip. Barbara says that when Dad raised chickens in New Jersey that he would always kill the last one before the trip. Mom would fry it and put it in the picnic for our drive to Vermont.

Besides the fried chicken there would be bread and butter, carrot and celery sticks, oranges and apples, Hershey chocolate candy bars, and fruit juice.

We would all pile in, the four sisters in the back and Mom and Dad in front.

* * *

My Dad was a smoker. He smoked Camel cigarettes all the way across the country and we weren't allowed to have the windows open. I always got carsick.

Mom didn't drive so Dad drove the whole way. In later years, he would let one of the four daughters drive when he got tired.

It would take us twenty-two to twenty-five hours from Illinois and we didn't stop unless it was to get gas. We girls learned good bladder control because we had to 'hold it' when we had to go to the bathroom until we got to a gas station.

We never stopped at a motel to sleep, just drove straight through. If Dad got tired at night he would pull into a cemetery or a churchyard and park the car. He would get out and take a blanket and sleep on the ground. I think Jeanne sometimes got out and slept on a blanket too. I didn't like sleeping in the car in a cemetery or churchyard. I would huddle close to my sisters trying to keep warm and ward off my fear of the dark.

* * *

The year I was seven my family was on their way to Vermont from Missouri and was driving in New York State near Rochester. This was before the throughway. It was late at night. Dad was tired so he pulled off the road into a cemetery where he could sleep.

Early the next morning he got up very early about 5 a.m. It was very foggy. He started the car and began to drive down the road. Suddenly a big animal came running across the road. It was a big horse and we hit it. It seemed to bounce on the hood of the car and then roll off. It actually got up and walked away.

The car however, was not so lucky. It did not move. Dad had to find a farmhouse to use a telephone. This was before cell phones. He called a garage that sent out a tow truck to get us. We were taken into the city of Rochester. We stayed in an apartment for three days while the car was getting repaired. I can still picture this ominous huge brick building in the middle of the city and still feel the humidity, heat and closeness of that apartment.

* * *

Mom's Shoe

I don't remember if this happened on that same trip but on one of those journeys driving across New York we stopped at a store near Watertown. Mom had taken off her shoes while we were driving along. Dad stopped at a store to buy some perishables such as milk, butter, etc. since we were getting near to our destination. Mom opened her door on the passenger side for a few minutes while Dad was in the store. When he came back and was ready to leave she shut her door. We left the parking area and headed on toward Vermont and camp.

Nearly an hour later Mom leaned down to put her shoes on. There was only one. Obviously, one had fallen out back in Watertown at that little store when she opened her door. She never got her shoe back because Dad thought it was too far to drive back.

* * *

No matter what state we were coming from we always drove straight across the country to Vermont and to our destination if Dad could stay awake. On occasion we would arrive late at night or into the wee hours of the morning. We would stay in the car and sleep and wait for someone to come or wait until the hour when we could get into the camp.

At one of the camps that we stayed in for several years I remember the key was hidden inside the electrical box. Once we were there Dad could find the key and we could get into the camp. On this occasion however, a little field mouse was crouched inside the electrical box. Dad was very careful to remove the tiny creature before taking out the key.

* * *

We rented many camps during those years: *the Maple Lodge* at the top of the hill, *the Bristol Lodge, Fleets Inn, This is the Limit (the Limit)* and a few camps across the bay on East Road.

* * *

When we stayed at *Fleets Inn* or *the Limit* my Dad would make my Mom and we four girls get out of the car at the top of the hill. Our car was so packed and heavy that it would hit bottom. The road of course was not in the best condition either.

At the end of the stay at these camps after Dad had packed to go we would walk to the top of the hill before we got in. Again the car would have dragged and hit bottom.

* * *

One year a camp on South Road was the only one available. When we arrived it wasn't ready so we had to spend the night at a farm on Thompson's Point Road. This farm belonged to Mr. and Mrs. Bucklin and overlooked Town Farm Bay.

* * *

The stories I will share of those years take place primarily during the years that we rented *This Is The Limit* owned by Mr. And Mrs. Miller (later Mrs. Orcutt) and *Fleets Inn*, on the hill down behind *Maple Lodge* and across the road from *Havarest*. Stanley Prescott owned the *Fleets Inn.*

When *Fleets Inn* burned down in the fall of 1962 my Mom called me. I was a sophomore in college. She said, "Margaret, *Fleets Inn* has burned." I sat down and wept.

* * *

PEOPLE WE KNEW

There were particular people who my family met and associated with during those summers while at camp: the owners of camps, other renters, and Vermont local characters that we met in stores, at church, and out on the lake while fishing.

* * *

At the bottom of the hill off North Road and to the left of *This Is The Limit (the Limit)* and below *Fleets Inn* was a beautiful well-kept camp once known as the Kingsland camp and owned by Mr. Samuel L'Hommedieu and his wife Elsie.

Mrs. L'Hommedieu, formerly Elsie Foote, was originally from Vergennes, Vermont. They lived in Washington D.C.

This delightful couple, were five years older than my Mom and Dad. These two couples befriended each other and spent many evenings through the years playing bridge. Mrs. L'Hommedieu and my Mom wrote to each other for many years.

The L'Hommedieu's had a little wooden boat that they would go out in. They and their two sons, Sam and Robert would go out in the boat on sunny days and motor over to the other side of Gardiner's Island in Hawkins Bay. There they would anchor and swim off the boat. They would often take a picnic with them. I knew this because I would watch them go off in their boat with a picnic basket and towels.

The L'Hommedieu camp being on the end of Long Point had a view of the lake on three sides - the west, north and east. I thought their location the best on the point because of the grand panoramic view of the lake. It began on the left from Swift's point and Diamond Island north and/or right sweeping across past what we always called Rattlesnake Mountain of the Adirondacks, on up the lake to Split Rock over to Thompson's Point and Flat Rock, to Town Farm Bay (where the Point Bay Marina is presently located) and the Dean's Islands, in Pleasant Bay. This was/ is still a magnificent view!

I also liked the rocky end and grassy area of this property filled in with various sizes and many shaped cedar trees. There was an old cedar that stuck out on one side that became my sister's and my favorite sitting place.

Through the years my sisters and I would walk out to the end of the point in front of the L'Hommedieu camp to lay on our towels, sun bathe and swim off the end of the point. We would swim over to 'the rocks.'

'The rocks' were rocks that stuck out of the water seventy-five to a hundred yards off shore.

* * *

When I tell people I meet today on Long Point that we swam off the end of the point those many years ago they seem astounded. They say, "We would never go there." And they ask, "How did you get permission?"

We four Berger girls always went out to the end of the point to swim. We went along the rock edge so as not to cut across the property of the L'Hommedieu's. We would get out on the rocks, lay our towels out, sun bathe, swim off the end, read our books and write in our journals. We never questioned that they would mind us being there. In later years when it did occur to us to ask, they were very happy to let us continue. We weren't noisy and we didn't cause any disturbance.

When I was in high school and my sisters were away, having gone to college and working summer jobs elsewhere, I would go and sit in Mrs. L'Hommedieu's kitchen. She would provide a cup of tea or coffee and we would chat.

One year, maybe it was two, in the late 1950's my oldest sister, Barbara, dated Sam their oldest son. I was impressed that she would be dating this young handsome lawyer from Washington D.C.

In the early 1960's when I was in college one of my friends, Carol from Ohio, came with my parents and me to Long Point. She too, dated Sam.

We also enjoyed the friendship of the younger son, Bob and his girl friend, Ruth, whom he later married. They now own the camp and are summer residents of Long Point where Mr. and Mrs. L'Hommedieu spent all those years. Bob and Ruth's children and grand children come to visit them in and continue to appreciate this beautiful location.

* * *

In August 1950 our family met Lorna. Lorna Dean was the youngest of three sisters: Malia, Arloa and Lorna. They lived with their parents during the summer in a camp located on the largest of three islands known as *the Dean's Islands* and/or *the Three Sisters*. These islands are to the north of Pleasant Bay and Long Point, and across the cove from Flint Beach and Thorpe's Point.

On the middle and largest of the islands there is a main house with a porch and three small one-room cottages. Each of the girls had their own little cottage to use.

Lorna's Dad, Professor Leon Dean was a professor of English, Short Story Writing, and Vermont History at the University of Vermont and the author of several Historical Fiction books for children.

Lorna's Mom, Hazel Dean, (Mrs. Dean to me), was a wonderful, vibrant, life-long Vermonter. When she passed away in June of 1996 she was just a couple of months short of her one hundred and one birthday.

* * *

On that bright, sunny day in 1950, when we met, Lorna was out in her canoe near the end of one of the islands. My Dad and I were in our small motorboat, trolling. Dad was fishing. He saw Lorna. He called out to her a greeting. Soon they were in conversation. He asked her if she wanted to climb Camel's Hump, with our family the next day.

This mountain, the second highest in Vermont stands high in the Green Mountain range and is seen from many spots when out on Lake Champlain and/or driving the highways of Vermont. Camel's Hump, is also known by old Vermonters as 'the couching lion.'

Lorna said, "Yes." She wanted to climb the mountain with us.

Thus began a friendship of Lorna, her Mom and Dad and the Berger family. Lorna and I, in particular have been friends for these many years.

When I was in college in Connecticut I would take the greyhound bus to visit her and on occasion I stayed at her folk's home on Prospect Street in Burlington, Vermont.

One year I stayed with them and went to the Ice Festival in February sponsored by the University of Vermont.

Other years after Lorna married Myron Brown, I would take the bus and stay at their home. In fact I was on a bus sitting in White River Junction, Vermont on my way to see them the day President Kennedy was shot in 1963.

Mike and Lorna lived in several different communities over the years. It was fun to see the different homes that they were either building or fixing over.

When I married my husband, Whitney, he and I would drive up to Vermont and spend an occasional weekend with them. There was a span of years when we did not see each other, both couples busy raising our families.

In recent years, Lorna, my Vermont 'sister' and I have once again had new fun-filled adventures together on our beloved lake.

* * *

Arnold Manchester, a math teacher from Mamaroneck, New York owned a camp on the point off of North Road facing the West across the lake toward New York State. *The Linden* is the camp just south of the one he owned and his uncle's camp *Rock Ledge* was next door to the north.

Mr. Manchester's camp had been in his family and was passed on to him by his parents. His Dad, Bob Manchester, owned a beautiful wood inboard 'the Wanderer' that Arnold inherited.

My remembrance of Mr. Manchester (Arnold) was watching him cross the bay in 'the Wanderer' standing up in the middle of this well-built classic boat. When 'the Wanderer' was no longer to be used, Arnold and his wife, Audrey, had it towed out to the 'broad' lake, had it filled with heavy rocks and allowed it to sink.

Arnold loved to sail and was known for his sailing exploits on the lake in the 'Aftermath', one of several sailboats that he owned. He was a math teacher, therefore, the appropriate name of 'Aftermath' for his boat.

He and his wife, Audrey, had married late in life. I found them to be an interesting couple to be with. I would sometimes enjoy a cup of tea with Audrey during my teenage years when my sisters were not around.

In August 1967 when my husband, Whitney, and I honeymooned at Long Point, Mr. Manchester took us out for a sail in one of his smaller sailboats. This was probably the last time I saw him.

* * *

The Stowe family owned their camp off North Road called *Lotta Water*. This camp originally named *the Burlington* was one of the first camps built during the tenting days of early campers.

The owner of *Lotta Water,* Karl Stowe and his wife, daughter, Margie, and son, Harold, long-time summer residents, were always at Long Point when our family came each August.

My sister, Barbara, tells how she would play with Margie when my folks rented the *Just A Mere* in the late 1930's. This was before I was born.

My remembrance of meeting the Stowe family was one August after my sister, Jeanne, walked to each of the camps on the point introducing herself and telling the summer people that she was going to have a birthday. She would say to them, "If there are any children at this camp they are invited to my party." Margie came to the party.

Harold Stowe and his wife, June, still own the camp and spend their summers there.

* * *

The Bay View Farm

Mr. Edward Oliver Danyow was the owner of the big farm off Bay View Road. He was the North Ferrisburgh Station Agent and telegraph operator for many years. His wife, Lydia, ran the store by the track crossing on Long Point Road during those years and later was a phone operator.

Sometimes my Dad would go to the Bay View farm to get worms. He would take one of us girls with him on occasion. I remember going to this farm with him.

We would park by the big barn and walk behind the house to a pasture that overlooked the lake at Pleasant Bay (also known as Kimball's Bay). We would go at dusk after the cows had been taken to the barn. We would go out and get these big, long, fat, squiggly worms called 'night crawlers'.

If the ground was dry we would pour a solution of mustard and water down the wormholes and that would get them up and out fast.

Mr. Danyow would come out and visit with my Dad. I was afraid of both of them, these two gruff men, but I liked to go and listen to them talk.

Our friend Lorna's family always used the Danyow dock and beach area to keep their boats that they used to get to and from their islands.

I didn't know way back then that fifty years in the future my husband and I would own a camp on leased property of this same farm.

* * *

Louis LaFlam Memorial Park

The part of Long Point known as the Louie LaFlam Memorial Park was once the area where the Community Building, tennis courts and shuffleboard court were located. There is still a tennis court there and in recent years a play area for young children.

Louis LaFlam had worked at the Ball farm for many years and did handyman jobs for the various campers and renters at Long Point. He married Helen Shortsleeves and bought the white house on the curve of the hill of Long Point Road. This house they made into a lovely home.

Mr. LaFlam raised chickens that he dressed and sold as well as fresh eggs and vegetables from his large garden.

Mr. Louis LaFlam as well as Mr. George Davis was also a caretaker of keys for the camps that my family rented.

I especially remember the flower gardens because of a flower I was given. Our family had just arrived to spend our vacation in a camp at Long Point. We had driven up the driveway of the LaFlam farm and Dad was talking to Mr. LaFlam. Mrs. LaFlam came out of the house to talk to my mother while Dad was talking to Louis. My sisters and I were sitting in the back seat of the Buick. She picked a pretty yellow flower and handed it to me. I was thrilled.

* * *

The Palmer's Garage the Forerunner of a Mini-Mart

Mr. Morris Palmer and his wife, Eleanor, ran a garage called Palmer's on Route #7 in North Ferrisburgh back when we rented camps on Long Point. My Dad used to stop there to get gas for the car, gas and motor oil for the boat, and cigarettes. He and Mr. Palmer would stand and chat, usually about fishing, while smoking their Camel cigarettes. My sisters and I would go in to buy a soda or candy.

Their store sold just about anything a camper might need from the 'nuts and bolts' of boat parts, motor oil, etc.; fishing equipment and night crawlers; a variety of small parts for farm machinery; to cigarettes and candy bars, etc. This little store was the forerunner of the mini-marts of today. Eleanor Palmer continues to run this little store.

* * *

Allie Murray's Garage

My Dad met Mr. Murray, Allie to us, when he patronized the gas station and car garage that Mr. Murray owned on Route #7 (now old Route #7 across the street and up the hill from the Congregational Church) in Charlotte.

The two men soon became fast friends because of their mutual interest in fishing, primarily trout fishing. Mr. Murray and his wife, Hazel lived in a wonderful white house with green shutters off Route 7 (now old Route #7) on the corner of Hinesburg Road.

They also owned a lease to a piece of property out on Thompson's Point. The property faced into Converse Bay and Cedar Island. There was no camp, but a large fireplace and picnic table for having grand outings. A stairway went down the side of the ledge to a rocky beach below.

Our two families had many wonderful chicken barbecues over the years. I remember the special marinade that Mr. Murray put on the chickens that were cut into halves and then cooked over a wood fire in the brick fireplace. We often made ice cream in a hand cranked ice cream maker.

On one occasion of these barbecues one of my sisters, I think Bobbie (Roberta), and I walked from Long Point to the Murray's property, about six/seven miles. I know it was a long walk, but we were young and able.

The Murray's son, Charles, and his wife, Shirley, reconnected with my family in thc last few years and we once again are enjoying picnics and outings together.

* * *

Heavy Foot

Charles tells the story of when his dad was riding with my Dad in our Buick. The two men were coming back from trout fishing by the old mill on Lewis Creek. My Dad was driving them down State Prison road just east of Monkton.

There is a long winding curve that goes down hill and is of rough dirt and gravel as it still is today. My Dad was known for his 'heavy foot' on the gas pedal and as they came around the bend and down this hill Mr. Murray thought for sure they were going to fly off the hill into the field. It is not hard for me to imagine his fear.

* * *

Vermont Pen-pal

Lynn Webster was a person I met as a pen pal through a church newsletter. I was ten years old, living in Illinois when I saw the letter from another little girl living in Burlington, Vermont. She wanted a pen pal and since I already had a love for Vermont I wrote to her.

Lynn, her brother, David, and parents lived on Willard Street, Burlington, Vermont.

We wrote to each other establishing a friendship that lasted for several years. In 1954 we met when Lynn's parents came to visit friends on Long Point in their speedboat. They brought Lynn with them and I came to meet her.

That summer we visited back and forth between their camp at Bartlett's Bay and our rented camp on Long Point. We took a ride on the Ticonderoga paddle wheel boat while it was still running on Lake Champlain. In 1959 we visited this historic vessel at the Shelburne Museum after it had been brought across land by railroad and given a permanent home.

While at the museum we took each other's picture with our heads in the stocks in front of the of old Castleton jail.

Lynn and I wrote to each other for several years through college. My husband, Whitney and I visited her in 1970 after she was married and living at Bartlett Bay with her husband and new daughter.

* * *

Mrs. Orcutt

Mr. Miller was the owner of *This Is The Limit (the Limit*). I don't remember him at all but I do remember when he died. And I remember when his widow married Mr. Orcutt.

At the time we were renting *Fleets Inn* up the hill from *the Limit*. Mrs. Miller asked my Dad to perform the ceremony of marriage for her and Mr. Orcutt. They got married right on the porch of the camp. Afterward they had a toast to the bride and groom. I wasn't there but I could see them from the screened in porch of *Fleets Inn*.

My Dad told us later that they had wine and he had held his glass behind his back and poured the wine out over the rocks. It seems silly to me that he would do this because we knew he did drink wine on occasion. I expect it was the image he wanted to create of who he was as a minister. I really don't think it would have made any difference.

Mrs. Orcutt and I got to know each other many years later after my husband and I bought our own camp in 1997. She and I visited several times at her camp before her death in 1998. Her granddaughter, Holly owns the camp now. My sister, Jeanne, and her family have made plans to rent it once again for September 2001.

* * *

Mr. Stanley Prescott owned *Fleets Inn.* Mr. Prescott was bald, had a mustache and wore suspenders. And he liked to drink a lot too. He and my Dad got along well. Sometimes my Dad would go visit with him in the years he lived in the old trailer up near the creamery on Long Point Road.

* * *

Favorite Camp—Fleet's Inn

The various camps that our family stayed in were usually near the water. *Fleets Inn* located just above the L'Hommedieu camp on the northeast end of the point was my favorite. I could draw a floor plan even today without any hesitation and know every nook and cranny.

In the front of the camp was a large screened-in porch that held an old wooden table, four ladder-back rockers, and had a north and east view of the lake. On rainy days the four sisters would often play cards at the table or read books sitting in thc rockers.

The eating area was small but included a highly glossed pine picnic table. The dishes were cranberry colored glass and the thick drinking glasses were a royal blue.

* * *

Dad's 'Green Thumb'

My Dad came to Vermont to fish but he also liked gardening and I would say had a 'green thumb.' He would go up in the mountains and bring back wild flowers: Columbine, Jack-in-the-pulpit, Solomon-seal, Johnnie-jump-ups, etc. and replant them into the side rock area of the *Fleet's Inn.* During the month we would be there he would create a beautiful, many colored rock garden.

* * *

Bristol Lodge one of the earliest camps built, located at the top of the hill, is one of two camps that I remember we stayed that were not on the water. The other was *Maple Lodge*. I stayed there with my Mom and Dad one summer when the three siblings were away at summer jobs.

A lot of spiders were in the upper room where I slept. I would make my bed each morning as if it were an envelope. At night I would slide inside the envelope and fold it over so that no spiders could get inside while I slept.

This camp the name changed to the *Friendly Croft* burned in October 1996 and has been rebuilt by Tom Paine and Shirley Reed of Charlotte, VT. Shirley did the architectural planning for it.

My husband and I have enjoyed seeing this new camp be built and the variety of bright colors that have been included in the trim. The driftwood rail on the porch spells out the name *Friendly Croft*.

* * *

Camp Activities

While staying on Long Point my sisters and I liked to walk on the rocks by the water, play hide and seek in the woods, lie out and sun bathe, and go for rides in the rowboat. We liked to go out in the motorboat with our Dad when he went fishing. Occasionally he would take the whole family out just for a ride it the motor boat and we would often go with him and take a picnic for an all day outing when he went trout fishing.

When we stayed at *the Limit* and played hide and seek we would sometimes climb up the ledge in back of the camp and jump over onto the roof. We would climb along the connector to the gazebo and lay flat in front hanging on to the top. We could hide from whomever was 'it.'

* * *

Follow the Arrow

Besides inside games such as a variety of Board games and Cards my sisters and I would often play games outside such as hide and seek and kick the can. We would use the community area for shuffleboard and softball. Sometimes we made up games that we played together with other children we met who lived and/or were renters on the point during the summer.

My sister Bobbie reminded me of one of them called 'Follow the Leader' or 'Follow the Arrow'.

The idea was to have one person, the leader, make a trail for the other participants to find and follow. The leader would have a ten-minute start. She/he would leave clues of arrows made with sticks, leaves, and/or rocks that would point the direction of the trail being made. The purpose was to follow the trail and eventually catch the leader.

Long Point is full of wooded areas, gravel roads, rock ledges and camps. The trail might lead through, around, and over and the arrows weren't always easy to see. 'Follow the Arrow' would often last for hours in order for each one playing would have a turn at being the leader. It was a great way to spend hours in fun with siblings and friends.

* * *

Long Point Camp Store

Two places of particular interest when we vacationed at Long Point were the Long Point store and the Community building.

The store was located in the camp now called *Sunset* on North Road across from the Patterson's camp, *Spindrift*, and north of Mrs. Thornton's camp. Various camp children worked in this store over the years and at some point in time the first telephone on the point was installed.

We didn't have to shop a lot because our family always brought the staples from home and produce from Dad's large vegetable garden. And for meat we ate fish: perch, pickerel, pike, large and small mouth bass, catfish, and even an occasional eel.

Previous to the opening of the store an ice-man used to come around to bring ice for the iceboxes that were in the various camps and a fresh produce man would walk around selling his wares of vegetables and berries. Mr. LaFlam came around often with fresh produce from his farm.

The little store carried staples: sugar, milk, bread, butter, etc. and, of course, ice cream, soda and such for the younger generation.

For several years one could buy the homemade pies made by a Mrs. Grady. I don't remember this but my older sisters do.

As kids it was fun to walk to the store from our camp for ice cream cones and/or when we needed to get some item for Mom.

After the store closed and became a privately owned camp we would walk the two miles to the railroad crossing on Long Point Road and the store there run by Mrs. Lydia Danyow.

* * *

Summer Community Gatherings

The Community building was a small brown building in the woods near the tennis court. Mr. Henderson, owner of *Cedar Ledge,* was a great tennis buff and kept the court in good repair.

My sisters and I liked to play shuffleboard on the court nearby and attend the family movie time and/or a magic show on Saturday night held in the community building.

On Sunday nights there would often be a hymn sing and, of course, we always went to that. These events were held outside the building on hot summer nights, but on rainy days we all went inside.

One summer when we rented a camp on East Road I met a girl, Kristina Sjellman, from Henniker, New Hampshire. She and I would play shuffleboard nearly every day.

On Saturdays there would often be potluck suppers before the movie at the community building. And I remember fireworks one year.

I know that it got pretty buggy so we wore long sleeve shirts and long pants for those evening events and covered our bodies with ointment.

The July Fourth picnic that is still held each year is a remnant event of those family times.

* * *

A Natural Sitting Spot

My sisters and I liked to walk on the rocks (meaning the shore that consisted of rock ledges and boulders) along the water's edge and would often go to sit and watch the water at our favorite spot on the L'Hommedieu property.

There by the old bent cedar tree that stands on the rocky ledge near the water facing west and north one can see the marvelous panorama of the lake.

This dear old tree had one branch that was shaped like a big old arm. That branch was not too far from the base and easily accessible for sitting. My sisters and I would often take our turn at sitting there in the arm of the tree and daydream or write in our diaries.

Through the years I have come back to this place to find peaceful contentment.

In the early 1990's when my daughter, Torrey, was a student at the University of Vermont I would drive her to school in Burlington. On the way home I would drive down Route #7 and come to Long Point. I would walk out to our old friend, the cedar tree and sit in its comforting arm.

In these recent years during our sister reunions my sisters and I have all been back to receive its comforting arm and remember.

* * *

Walking the Rock Ledges

One of the walks I remember best was when my sister, Bobbie, (Roberta) and I were still elementary school age.

This particular summer she and I spent much time together and we would walk a great deal. We would take sandwiches made of white Wonder bread with a mixture of a processed cheese called Velveeta, raisins and mayonnaise.

We would walk and explore and when we got hungry we would sit on the rocks and eat our sandwiches. This was a very special time for me with her.

A few years later when Bobbie had a boy friend, Freddie, from Hackensack, New Jersey, I was very jealous. She would go off with him in his little white dinghy. I wanted those times with her, the exploring of the rock ledges, the eating of cheese sandwiches back.

* * *

Rokeby Museum

My Dad always got his fishing license at the Town Clerk's Office in Ferrisburgh, VT. During those early years that office was in the town clerk's home on Route # 7. I remember going up the long driveway to the top of the hill with my Dad in his old black Buick to this large Victorian style house. This property is today known as the Rokeby Museum.

Founded as a museum by Leon Dean the Rokeby Museum shares the history of a remarkable Quaker Family, the Robinson's who were active in the Underground Railway during the Civil War. Rokeby was their home for several generations from the 1790s to 1961.

Each August the museum staff and volunteers host an Ice Cream and Pie Social on a Sunday afternoon. This is a great way to share the history of this illustrious family and to gather community and summer tourists and/or residents into a time of fellowship.

* * *

Fishing With Dad

All of the sisters would take turns going fishing with my Dad out on the lake. There was a sixteen-foot aluminum boat with a 6 HP motor on it that we went in to go out on the lake. Dad would get up early about 5:30 a.m. and whichever one of us was going would get up too. They would go out in the boat for a couple of hours and then come back for breakfast. My Dad would make oatmeal with the delicious extras of melted butter, brown sugar and real whole milk and then wake everyone up to eat together.

My sister, Jeanne, went out with him the most to fish because she was the tomboy. I was next as the tomboy. We didn't mind watching Dad clean the fish, cut the head off, etc. In fact we learned how to do this too.

I liked to watch especially when the head was cut off because you could see the heart still beating. We did not mind putting the worm on the hook either if we were asked too. The other two sisters were squeamish about this.

* * *

The Small-Mouthed Bass

One vacation when Barbara and I were the only two siblings at camp Dad would take us fishing with him. We would often go out to Hawkin's Bay behind Gardiner's Island and just drift. Dad would fish and Barbara and I would have books to read.

On one of these little expeditions Dad was fishing and his line all of a sudden began to jerk. He quickly pulled and we all realized something 'big' was hooked. He wanted Barbara to have the net ready. Neither of us was ready for whatever creature was at the end of the fishing line.

Dad hauled in the line. Reaching out he pulled the end of the line in and there was a beautiful, large, small-mouth bass. This was a delight to my Dad and exciting.

All of this took place so fast. Barbara was supposed to reach out with the net so Dad could put the fish right in it. Well, I don't know what happened but as Dad unhooked the fish it slipped out of his hand. Of course it had been fighting and squirming the whole time. It did not want to be caught. The net that Barbara was holding was not in place. The fish got away!

You might imagine that our Dad was upset and in fact there were a few unsavory words and comments from him to us.

* * *

Catching My First Fish

The first time I ever caught a fish I was four or five years old - that meant it was 1947/48. It was off the rocky ledge outside the back door of *This Is The Limit*.

I would sit out there sometimes and watch the water and see little fish swim by. My Dad gave me a small pole he had made from a branch and had tied a string with a hook and a piece of a night crawler (a large fat worm). I threw it in the water and almost right away something pulled the line. I quickly pulled the line (string) up but there was nothing on it, not even the worm.

Inside the camp I knew there was a piece of fat left over from some meat from the night before. I went and got it and stuck it on the hook. I threw my line in again and sat to wait. Within a few seconds the line began to wiggle. I waited just a second or two the way my Dad had told me and before it could pull away I gave it a jerk and got it up and out of the water. I had caught a little perch probably not more than four or five inches long. I was so excited. I was 'hooked' from then on thinking, of course, that I would make a great fisherman. My Mom fried it for me for lunch.

* * *

Catching/Eating Fish

I can't remember when Dad didn't catch any fish whether it was large or small mouth bass, pickerel, walleyed pike, perch, or catfish from the lake or trout from the New Haven or the Mad River, Lewis or Otter Creeks. We always seemed to have them for dinner.

My Dad would clean the fish with Jeanne helping and my Mom would fry it in a big black skillet. Sometimes she would make a breading to roll the fish in first.

On occasion we also had fried lake eel that Dad had caught over near the Dean's Islands. Even though they were greasy, I liked the sweet taste of them.

In recent years I have found out through my sister, Jeanne, that my Dad didn't like fish. He ate it she says, but he once told her he never liked it. He just liked to catch them.

* * *

Mom's Enjoyment or Not?

I have always wondered if my Mom really enjoyed going to Vermont. She probably did because she knew the rest of us were having a good time. But she worked hard while we were at camp. She had to cook, clean, and do laundry just like at home. And at camp she did most of the laundry by hand.

She did not enjoy swimming or going in the boat and I know she worried when any of us were out on the lake in the motorboat with dad and/or rowboat. She would take us to the bay when we were small to paddle around in the water but she was fearful the whole time. She shared with me years after that she had almost drowned twice while she was in college.

She would go out in the boat on occasion only after much coaxing from my Dad.

* * *

Hazardous Boating

I heard this story of a boating excursion my family had before Bobbie and I were born, probably during the late 1930's. My Mom, Barbara, Jeanne and Dad went out in the small flat-bottomed aluminum boat to go fishing over near Kingsland Bay.

They were there trolling along the shore for a while when a sudden wind came up on the lake which soon turned into a full-blown storm. My Dad started the little 6 HP motor up but the boat didn't go far before a wave washed over it and the engine conked out.

My Dad had my Mom and two older sisters, small children at the time, lay down flat in the boat. Dad let the boat drift in the wind that fortunately went toward the southwest and the sand beach where the Ferrisburgh town beach is now. They waited out the storm. My Dad got the motor to work again and they went back along the shore's edge around MacDonough's Point, into Hawkin's Bay and on to Long Point.

* * *

The Bait

In order to go fishing you have to have bait. My Dad would use either night crawlers (big worms) or minnows. My Dad wouldn't buy night crawlers unless absolutely necessary. He would go get them. He would go at night when they were up and out of the ground, especially after a rainstorm. He would take his flashlight and shine it on the ground looking for holes. If the worms were not out he would pour a mixture of mustard and water down the hole. Whether rain or mustard solution you had to be ready to reach down quickly and grab these long squiggly, slimy creatures.

The best places to go for night crawlers were churchyards, cemeteries, and cow pastures. We would go to the Danyow farm, the pasture by the old Ball farm, to the Catholic churchyard and/or the high school grounds in Vergennes.

Minnows Dad would get from Mr. Jim McDurfee on Greenbush Road. He was a fishing guide for the State of Vermont but raised minnows too. I liked going with Dad to see this tall, twinkled-eyed black man.

I enjoyed listening to their men's conversation as we walked back to the little creek behind his house. This is where the minnows were kept in large wire mesh boxes.

* * *

Tubing the Waves

We stayed over on the East side of the Bay on what is today known as East Road for two or three years. We stayed at the camp between *Cedar Rest* and the camp once owned by the Pidgeon family.

In 1954 the water in the lake was very high due to hurricane, *Carol.* The water had also turned brown which is quite a feat when you consider its length of one hundred and fifteen miles, ten-mile width in some places and its considerable depth. The discoloration had apparently come from silt and sands being stirred up.

In August while we were there it rained a lot and the wind was blustery and waves on some days were several feet high.

My sisters and I with permission from our Dad took huge inner tubes to ride the waves. One of the tires was from a tractor so it was quite large. My Mom was not happy that we were going out in the wind and waves but my Dad said okay. My mother had cause to worry about us out there, but we didn't think about getting scared or that it might be dangerous. And my Dad had tied a long thick rope to these tires and tied it to the lamp pole on the rocky point.

My sisters and I felt tremendous excitement and I am sure thought it great fun riding the waves!

* * *

A Turtle Story

One morning that same summer a large turtle washed up on the rocks by our camp. My Dad captured it, because it couldn't get back into the water.

A man from the Vermont State Environment Department came after my Dad called. He said that by its size and the length of the slimy green moss growing on its back that the turtle was probably over a hundred years old.

Later in the week my sisters and I were upset when we found out that the man had not taken the turtle to put back in the lake but had killed it for turtle soup. This is what our Dad told us.

* * *

Love of the Lake

All the days were joyous for me and I believe my sisters would agree, too, while staying at camp on Lake Champlain, no matter what the weather, that special place of my childhood and theirs.

I loved warm, sunny days with a calm lake. But I also liked the sunny, blustery, windy days when the white caps moved across the lake.

On rainy, stormy days when it would thunder and lightning it would bring excitement and adventure into play. I liked to stand on the screened-in porch of the *Fleets Inn* or in the gazebo of *the Limit* and listen to the wind, watch the rain come down and the high waves lap the shore.

The electricity would go out and candles would have to be lit. We had a fireplace or wood stove in some of the camps and Dad would make a fire using folded up newspapers and wood. We would be cozy and warm. On some of those rainy days my sisters and I would play cards: Canasta and War. Sometimes we would each curl up on our bed or a sofa and read.

* * *

Trout Fishing Excursions

My Dad enjoyed going out in the motorboat to fish on the lake but I believe that what he liked best was to go trout fishing on a mountain stream.

He would go with his friend Mr. Murray and others but sometimes he would take my Mom, the sisters and me. There are two places I remember in particular that we went.

Just outside of Bristol, Vermont to the east there is a place where the New Haven River comes along between rocky cliffs. There was an old viaduct there and down below a waterfall, known as Bartlett Falls. My Dad in his long waders, fishing jacket and hat, carrying his pole and tackle box would walk across the viaduct and down the embankment on the other side of the river to fish.

While he fished we girls would go to a big pool farther down to wade. We would build sand castles along side the river and explore the woods. My Mom would put down a blanket, sit and watch us, write letters, and read.

The other location was on the Middlebury River near Middlebury Gap just above East Middlebury off Route # 125. There is a little side road that goes off this main road. Dad would park the car and go down the hillside to a place where there is a deep gorge.

Of course there were lots of places along these picturesque rivers but those two were the favorite spots.

Other favorite spots I remember were places on Lewis Creek, little Otter Creek that were easy to get to from Route #7, and the Otter Creek that comes into Vergennes.

Whenever we went on one of these trout fishing adventures my Mom always brought wonderfully delicious picnics that she had prepared. There would be cold fried chicken, hard-boiled eggs, juicy red tomatoes, slices of white cheddar cheese and white bread. She would always bring some kind of delicious cake or cookies and juice, iced tea and/or lemonade.

It seemed Dad would always catch enough trout to bring home to have for dinner. I liked the fish that my mom would deep fry but my favorite part was the adventure of the outing.

* * *

Swimming—Favorite Places

All four of us girls liked to swim. Our Mom was not a swimmer, but our Dad encouraged us. Our Mom was willing to walk down to the bay with us when we were small so that we could wade and then begin to swim. I don't remember who taught me and/or any of us but we all did learn.

None of us really liked the bay area because of the weeds and mushiness of the sand and/or mud bottom. There were leeches, (We called them bloodsuckers too), and once one of them got on one of the sister's leg. My Dad used an old German knife to cut it out.

When we were older we began walking out to the end of the point to swim off the rocks by the L'Hommedieu's property. We also swam off the rocks in front of the *Fleets Inn* where Arloa and Frank Leary now have their dock to the Dean's Islands.

When we rented the *Maple Lodge* at the top of the hill we got into the habit of walking down in front of *the Princeton* to the cliff. I recollect Dad diving off at the top of the cliff. We girls would go down lower along the side of the cliff and lay out our towels. We could then step into the water onto pieces of the cliff that stuck out of the ledge under water. Then we could push off to swim. It was deep there, over our heads about ten to twenty feet. You had to know how to swim.

Once when I was small, perhaps seven or eight, maybe younger, I went out in an inner tube from the cliff. I didn't realize how far I had gotten. Anyway I either fell off or let go of the inner tube and it began to float away from me. I must have panicked because my sister, Roberta (Bobbie), saw that I was going to go under. She swam out to get me back to safety.

* * *

Summer Romance

One year while I was still in high school I had my first summer romance in Vermont. My Mom, Dad and I had come to Long Point without the sisters who were all working at jobs.

The Henderson family who owned *Cedar Ledges* on the north west-end of Long Point was from Connecticut. Bob their son and I met. I had known of him for several years.

He and I would meet at the cliff in front of their camp. We would lie out on our beach towels and we would swim entering the water from the cliff. We would sun bathe and talk. Sometimes we would take walks and hold hands. I was absorbed in teenage romance.

I had to be careful because I didn't know what my parents would do or say. I was pretty sure my Mom would not think anything bad, but I was afraid of my Dad's reaction.

* * *

Sunday Excursion

On Sunday mornings while vacationing in Vermont my family would drive to Charlotte so that we could attend church at the Congregational Church on Route #7. I believe it is now old Route # 7 and/or Old Church Road.

I liked those Sunday excursions especially after the church service. My Dad would take me with him to walk up into the cemetery on the side of the hill behind the church. He and I would take time to read the epitaphs on the gravestones, especially the old ones.

One Sunday we saw a most unusual epitaph on a tombstone from the early 1800's. It is one I have never forgotten and like to tell people about it. The epitaph on it says, *"Here lies Abigail. She always did."* Perhaps this was the beginning of my love for genealogy research.

* * *

The Ticonderoga

In 1959 the last paddle wheel steamboat on Lake Champlain, the Ticonderoga was taken overland by a special laid train track to the Shelburne Museum in Shelburne, Vermont. It would be the largest exhibit to date.

This steamboat made daily trips up and down the lake for many years. And for many years early on it stopped to take on passengers from Thompson's Point. This was before my time.

I had opportunity to be one the passengers on its last lake voyage before it was taken to the museum. My friend, Lynn's folks, took Lynn and me on this historic event. Later that summer we went to the museum to see it in its new home.

At Shelburne Museum there are all kind of wonderful historical exhibits of early Vermont and New England life.

* * *

The Lake / The Green Mountains

All Long Pointers have some connection to Lake Champlain by boating, swimming, water skiing, fishing, canoeing, etc. and/or just being there to enjoy its ever-changing beauty.

Many of the people at Long Point also come to Vermont to enjoy the mountains especially the range of mountains known as the Green Mountain National Forest.

* * *

Climbing Camel's Hump

My family would go to the mountains so my Dad could find a stream to trout fish in. But we also liked to take hikes along the Long Trail part of the nations' Appalachian Trail.

One of our favorite trips that we took nearly every year was to hike up Camel's Hump or as some older Vermont folks call it 'the couching lion'.

Our mother would get up early on the designated day and fill a picnic basket with delicious food. There would be sandwiches of cold meats, cheeses and tuna fish salad, pickles, tomatoes, celery and carrot sticks, and cake or cookies for dessert. Sometimes she would fry chicken a day a head to take for eating cold with our fingers. She would bring jars of juice and a thermos of coffee for our Dad.

The six of us, Mom, Dad, and the four sisters would all pile into the Buick. Dad would drive over to Hinesburg, Vermont by way of Monkton. Then we would head East to Huntington Station, a small town at the base of the mountain. There a dirt road led us up into the mountains to the Burrows cottage. There, next to their house we would park our car and unload.

Our Dad led the way up the mountain with our Mom in tow. He would always find a big branch or pole that he held onto and she onto the other end.

My sisters and I would always find a place on the trail where we could get by our Dad and climb on a head. Every once in awhile there would be a tree across the trail and we would go under or over it. Sometimes we would stop to sit and rest and look out at the view of the other mountain ranges.

A stream would often be seen either crossing our trail or coming down the mountain along side the trail. We would stop and dip our hands down into the cold, crisp water and take a drink.

I remember a big flat rock that was in one of the streams at a wide spot and we would stop there to rest.

For several years a large uprooted tree that had fallen beside the trail, covered with soft green moss, gave us a place to rest and wait for our parents.

The hike to the top of Camel's Hump about 2.4 miles would take us about three hours.

Once at the top of the mountain, the summit, my sisters and I would run here and there and exploring the various rock areas. Our Dad would explore too and for a few years we were fortunate to find and pick blueberries. We would eat handfuls of these large succulent berries. But we would also take back to camp enough of them for Mom to make a scrumptious blueberry pie.

Our Mom would usually spread out a blanket and place the picnic things. She would sit and write letters and post cards to friends and/or read.

There was a wreckage of a plane down on the side of the mountain. It lay on a ledge several hundred feet below. One year Dad climbed down and found a small piece that he gave to one of us for a souvenir.

I have always enjoyed seeing Camel's Hump because I have such pleasant memories of my family there. In its height one can see it from all the various directions; from out on the lake and on the many highways and byways.

* * *

Continued Visits to Vermont

After my sisters and I were no longer living at home my parents continued going to Vermont on a regular basis for perhaps another five years until 1968. The older sisters now married would visit them in Vermont with spouses and/or grandchildren.

I have pictures of some of the grandchildren taken at *This Is The Limit* in 1964 and 1965.

In 1967 my husband and I rented a camp for our honeymoon and shared it with my parents. In 1968 I came to Long Point with a friend for a week.

In the early 1970's when my sister, Roberta (Bobbie), owned a camp off East Road, my parents had opportunity to come to Vermont for visits.

Figure 1 The Early Years - Dad Berger with fish, 1936; Mt. Philo, Charlotte, VT; Dad Berger and Barbara in boat; Mom (Frances B. Berger) with the daughters: Jeanne, Margaret, Barbara, and Roberta, 1948.

Figure 2 The Early Years - The author, Margaret, at age 4, sitting on the rocks of the Limit Camp; Jeanne with fish, 1954; Dad Berger and Barbara with fish, 1959; Dad Berger (Robert B. Berger) with the daughters, Jeanne, Margaret, Barbara, and Roberta, 1948.

Figure 3 The Early Years - Shirley Murray; Chicken barbecue at the Murray lot; A trout fishing spot; The First Congregational Church, Charlotte, Vermont.

Figure 4 The Early Years - Smuggler's Notch; Ticonderoga Paddle Wheel Boat at Shelburne Museum, 1959; Lynn Webster on the Ticonderoga; Margaret Berger (Morse), the author, in stocks.

Figure 5 Leon and Hazel Dean, 1980 (Courtesy of Lorna Dean Brown)

PART III

THE YEARS 1967—1997

MORSE FAMILY VERMONT LIFE EXPERIENCE

I met my husband, Whitney Doane Morse, of Guilford, Connecticut in the fall of 1966. Through the winter of 1967 we were in the middle of our courting period when I suggested a trip to Vermont. I wanted Whitney to drive me to Vermont so I could introduce him to Long Point on Lake Champlain. We drove up in the middle of February.

There was a lot of snow on the ground. We were able to drive as far as the bay where we parked the car by the little Ferrisburgh Community Park. I insisted that he walk me out to the end of the point. Neither of us had boots but we did it anyway. It was cold, and the snow was at least a foot high, but it was grand!

The area of Long Point on the shore of Lake Champlain is beautiful in summer, but the quietness and serenity of the white covered landscape in winter was spectacular!

* * *

Whitney and I were married on August 5, 1967 in the First Presbyterian Church, Bellaire, Ohio where my Dad was the minister. We were married in that grand brick church with my three sisters and my dear friend, Judy as attendants.

We left immediately after the wedding reception for our honeymoon. We drove across country through northern Pennsylvania into New York and across to New England and to our rented camp on Long Point, North Ferrisburgh, Vermont.

I had rented Mrs. Thornton's camp on North Road for two weeks. One week was for us, the honeymoon couple. The other week was for my Dad and Mom.

* * *

The Honeymoon

We arrived on a warm sunny day in the early evening. We had stopped for an overnight on the way and then for an early dinner in New York State near Crown Point.

Once we arrived at Long Point we had to get the key to the Thornton camp from George Davis, a longtime resident of Long Point. He and his wife, Vi, were caretakers of many camp keys during that period.

After we unpacked our clothes at the camp we had the evening to walk around the point, allow me to reminisce long ago family times, and to enjoy just being together. This walk was more pleasant for the feet since there was no snow.

We stopped and chatted with Arnold (Arnie) Manchester who was there with Audrey at their camp. Now that I was an adult and married I felt I could call Mr. Manchester, Arnie, as others did. He invited us to take a sail in his small sailing vessel the next day.

We sat on the rocks across from the camp and watched a spectacular sunset.

* * *

The first night and day at Long Point were wonderful!

I had gotten up and made my new husband scrambled eggs and bacon, buttered toast and coffee. We sat on the screened-in porch to eat our first cooked meal as newly weds. Then we walked to the Manchester's to go for that promised sail.

The two or three hours we had out in Arnie's sailboat proved to be marvelous. There was a good wind. There is not anything like being out on that lake. We sailed out and along the shore past Gardiner's Island into Hawkins Bay and around the point passed the French School, now Kingsland Bay State Park and past Swift Point. We headed across the 'broad' lake to the New York side heading north passed Rattlesnake Mountain and Split Rock back across to the Vermont side and around the several islands in Converse Bay. We then headed back going south and east around Thompson's point. I had always called these two points little and big Thompson's points, but little Thompson's has also been called Flat Rock.

Even though I had visited with Audrey for an hour at a time at their camp, I had never been in Arnie's presence more than five or ten minutes. Now I had two or so hours and learned what a fascinating character he was.

Whit and I got back to our honeymoon camp in mid-afternoon and had a late lunch. We then went outside across the road to sit on the rocks and just enjoy being together. I mused at how fantastic it was to be in Vermont in my favorite place and to also be there with my new husband!

* * *

Then the unexpected occurred.

I had rented the camp for Whit and I for our honeymoon of one week.

I had rented it for a second week for my parents. Well, instead of arriving the second week, my Dad and Mom arrived the second day.

While we were sitting on the rocks basking in the sun and taking in the view of the lake a car drove up next to ours, a black Buick. My Dad came down to where we were sitting and said, 'Here we are.'

Needless to say I was furious. I can look back now and laugh, but at that moment when they arrived I was definitely not happy. Whit and I packed our things and left. We drove back to Connecticut to our newly purchased home in Guilford. We spent our honeymoon week working in our new home. My Dad and Mom had their week and most of ours.

I have shared that story many times!

* * *

Island Camp

In August 1968, my Dad and Mom rented a camp on the little island off South Road of Long Point for two weeks. Mr. Edward Oliver Danyow owned this camp. In recent years his daughter has owned it.

Two days before my parents were to begin their trip from Ohio to Long Point, Vermont my Dad had to go to the hospital. He had kidney stones. My Mom and he were not able to travel to Vermont and use this camp.

Dad called us from the hospital. Did we want to use the camp on the island? Perhaps he was trying to make up for showing up on our honeymoon. I like to think so.

Whit couldn't get time off from his job at such short notice. But since I was a teacher and wasn't working in the summer I could go to Vermont and take advantage of this offer. I asked my friend, Judy, also a teacher, whose husband, Fran was away in Vietnam to go with me. The two of us drove to Vermont and used the camp.

My sister, Jeanne, and her husband, Paul, were on Long Point renting a camp on South Road for part of the time we were there so we spent time with them too.

Jeanne and I went out fishing up little Otter Creek. We were ecstatic after we caught a small-mouthed bass. We put it in a bucket to show off to the neighbors.

I don't remember very much about that week except the fishing and that Judy and I had fun in the little island camp. I have a picture of us standing in front of Whit's Porsche convertible that we drove to Vermont. We were returning the camp key to Mr. Lewis La Flam and were parked in his driveway.

* * *

In the fall of 1969 I was pregnant with our first child, due in December. Whit and I decided to take a drive up to Vermont for the weekend. We invited his Mom and Dad to come along. We would stay all night in a small two-room cottage on the side of Mt. Philo. Our friends, Lorna and Mike, were then owners of the Mt. Philo Inn, Charlotte, Vermont and they rented us the little cottage.

We of course had to go to Long Point and share this marvelous spot with Mom and Dad Morse. We went out on Saturday afternoon and took the walk around the point. We got to *Rock Ledge* the camp owned by Arnold Manchester's Uncle. We walked down to the front of this camp and sat looking at the water.

Even though it was October, it was a fairly warm day. I couldn't resist. I had to get in the water. Mind you, I was seven months pregnant and quite large up front. I had worn my swimsuit under my maternity dress. I took the pullover dress off and walked down to the water and right in to it. I am sure my husband and his parents thought me quite strange.

I stayed in the water only a few minutes, but I have never regretted going in the water that day. And I have always attributed the fact that our daughter, Torrey while she was a child, liked to swim under water to this experience!

* * *

Whit and I did not get back up to Long Point until the summer of 1972. We had taken trips to Vermont visiting other places of interest for a day or two but not to Lake Champlain. We had traveled up Route #100 and visited the Country Store in Weston. We had been to visit friends in Newfane, Vermont and taken a one-day drive for foliage in southern Vermont one autumn.

We were parents now to two precious little girls: Torrey, and Jessica.

* * *

My sister, Roberta (Bobbie), and her husband, Bob, had bought a camp on Long Point in the early 1970's. Bobbie and her two children Kenneth and Barbie would go and spend the summer. My parents would drive to Vermont and visit her for several days in August.

Our two daughters, Torrey and Jessica, were toddler and infant when we visited this camp for a couple of days in August 1972.

Jeanne, Paul and their children, Lori, Wesley and Jenny, were there too.

* * *

On one of those days I was still nursing our newest daughter, Jessica. So when Whit, Paul, and Jeanne went for a walk they took Torrey. They walked down East Road and out toward the end of the point. They stopped to look at the water and to rest on the cement dock owned by the Gardiner Island people.

When they returned from their walk they all had a story to tell. Apparently Torrey, then two and a half years old, had stepped off the dock and sank down into the water. Whit and Paul froze just looking down at her. Jeanne immediately lay down flat on her stomach, reached down and pulled Torrey up by her hair. Torrey was fine, unhurt and not upset. She told me about it when they returned to camp as if this experience was just a part of their walk. Then the adults told me what had occurred.

* * *

Motel Vacation

As our daughters grew older we did not get to Long Point often. My sister had sold her camp in the mid-1970s so there was no family connection and many of the camps that were once rented no longer were available.

For a few years we drove up to Vermont for occasional weekends finding a motel to stay in as we meandered north. The most memorable weekend was when we drove up one summer with no plan. The girls were five and seven.

We ended up at the Yankee Doodle Motel on route #7 in Shelburne, Vermont. It had begun raining on the way up from Connecticut and continued to do so the for the whole weekend.

We stuck it out staying in the motel playing cards and eating Vermont cheddar cheese and white bakery bread from the Vermont Country Store in Rockingham, Vermont.

Torrey and I went to church at the little Brownstone Episcopal Church in Shelburne. This church was founded and built by the Webb family. We ate two meals at a little diner along Route #7 in South Burlington.

* * *

Smuggler's Notch

One year Whit, the girls and I drove up to Stowe, Vermont to visit the Smuggler's Notch area. I had visited this mountain cavern several times with my family as a child.

We owned a gray Peugeot sedan. The car was diesel with a heavy engine in front. I remember that it hardly made the climb up the mountain to the top of the notch.

We also visited the Von Trapp lodge and other tourist attractions in the area of Mt Mansfield.

* * *

Visits to East Montpelier, VT

A dear friend of mine, Mural Markham and her husband, Fred, from Guilford, Connecticut owned a house in East Montpelier, Vermont. It was a lovely old brick farmhouse, a late 1800 vintage. In the mid- 1980's I would go up to visit them by myself on a weekend in the summer.

Fred and I would get up at 5 a.m. and we would walk together. We would walk the property line through the woods through an old apple orchard. We would see deer on occasion and their dog would chase after them. When we came back to the house Muriel would have coffee ready for us and then make us a wonderfully delicious breakfast.

Some mornings you could look through the window and see several deer eating apples off the tree right in the back yard. I wanted to reach out and touch them.

Muriel and I would go out to tag sales on Saturday mornings when I was visiting and sometimes we would see deer along the road. Some evenings she and I would take a drive along the country roads at dusk to look for them.

* * *

One year our family used the farmhouse when Muriel and Fred weren't there. We enjoyed walking the property and taking drives through the Northeast Kingdom. We found a little lake that we could swim and take rides in a rented canoe.

On one of these occasions when driving to this lake, Jessica spotted a large male deer, with huge antlers standing in a clearing. We were surprised to see it because it was mid-morning. Later when we returned from our trip to the lake, the buck was there again and Jessica was the one to spot it.

We always enjoyed eating dinner at a family oriented local diner on Route#2 whenever we traveled to East Montpelier.

* * *

Torrey, Jessica and I have T-shirts from the East Montpelier Country store. They visited the Markham's with me several times on a weekend when Whit couldn't go with us.

Muriel's grandson, David was there on one of those visits. He and the girls had a great time exploring the neighbor's big old, red barn.

* * *

Mom, Daughters, and Friends

The girls and I each brought a friend with us on a trip to East Montpelier when the Markhams were not there. My friend, Evelyn Linskey, went as my guest; Karen Scott, went as Torrey's friend; and Margaret Dolan came with Jessica. We drove up on a Friday afternoon and stayed two nights and two whole days.

The girls had fun exploring the barn, going on walks around the farm grounds, taking drives with Evelyn and me to look for deer and visiting the East Montpelier Country Store.

Margaret's Mom had given Evelyn and me a bottle of wine, Blue Nun. The second night we drank it. I think I drank most of it. We walked around the cow pasture in the dark laughing and giggling. The four girls thought we were silly. And we were! Evelyn had to put me to bed that night.

* * *

Trips to Maine

For several summers also during the 1980's instead of going to Vermont, Whit, the girls and I took a week's vacation staying in a camp on the shore of Lake Sebago in Maine. We took our canoe for excursions on that cold, clear inland lake.

A couple of summers we rented a small two-room cabin in Columbia, Maine up off the coast and owned by a distant Torrey relative, Betty Torrey.

We drove up to the summer home of former President Roosevelt at Campobello, Maine stopping to visit Bar Harbor, the Acadia National Park and Scootic Point.

The idea was to form our own memories as a family in a new and different place. Maine has its own varied beauty and these years were fun and wonderful, but we missed Vermont.

* * *

Vermont Education

In 1987 and 1989 our two daughters graduated from high school. When they chose college they both chose schools in Vermont. Torrey attended the University of Vermont, Burlington, Vermont and Jessica went to Castleton State

College, Castleton, Vermont. I was excited because I now had opportunity to return to this beloved state.

During those college years of our daughters my husband and I traveled back and forth numerous times and often visited Long Point going or coming to their colleges. Even if it was for an hour or two out of my way, I was glad to have these opportunities to drive to, be near and walk along the shore of the lake.

We explored other areas of the state driving the length of Route #100 and the length of Route #30. In those summers both girls had summer jobs so Whit and I took weekend trips to the Northeast Kingdom and various lakes up in the northern part of the state.

We rented a cabin on a little river on the border of Vermont and New Hampshire and visited the Franconia Notch area and the Old Man of the Mountain in New Hampshire where my family had once visited.

We were amazed at the new highway development of I-93 in this area, and developed in a way to retain the beauty of this part of New Hampshire. We bought a video that shares the history of the Franconia Notch area, the White Mountains and the development/building of the highway.

In different years we took the Steam Train from Bellows Falls to Chester and a train ride to see the autumn colors from the Procter quarry up into the mountains. Both of these train rides were happy times and we got to see a lot of Vermont's historic covered bridges and rivers as well as the beautiful countryside.

Eventually we returned to vacationing on Lake Champlain at Long Point.

* * *

Return to Long Point

In the summer of 1996 Whit and I decided that we would make arrangements to rent a camp on Long Point again. We made some inquires and through my friend, Lorna Dean Brown, we were introduced to Jane Kirsch. Jane owns the *Thistldo* off East Road and *Elmwood* off Annex Road of Long Point.

Jane rented *Elmwood* to us for a week in July.

This camp was charming. It had a fireplace, a built-in porch and deck. A rowboat and canoe were available for our use and a dock that we could swim off.

Lorna and Mike biked down to see us from their home on Route #7 in Charlotte visiting us at camp a couple of evenings. We shared a meal that they brought one night and we also went to the Old Dock Restaurant, Essex, New York via the Charlotte ferry.

I was thrilled to once again have opportunity to be out on the lake, walk along the roads of Long Point and take drives up into the mountains.

* * *

A Wedding

In the fall of 1996 our youngest daughter, Jessica, married Dan Hoey in Connecticut. My three sisters now living in the states of California, Illinois and Virginia traveled to Guilford for the wedding. Following this festive occasion that lasted several days the four sisters had a reunion.

* * *

Sister Reunion in Vermont

I had made arrangements with Jane Kirsch for my sisters and me to rent *Elmwood* the week following the wedding.

We left on a Sunday afternoon the day after the wedding, in my 1986 red Honda. Leaving on Sunday was for us just like those days as children when we came to Long Point, always leaving on a Sunday after church. We had a blast together.

* * *

I gave this poem with a collage of pictures to my sisters for Christmas that year. This poem shares our week together.

October 20th - 27th, 1996

A VERMONT JOURNEY!

A Vermont journey with sisters
    Barbara, Jeanne, Bobbie, the three.
This, an incredible week,
    For them and for me.

Driving through rain and stormy winds galore,
    Our anticipation bursting all the more.
Arriving Sunday, October twenty,
    We began a reunion of fun a-plenty.

Each day filled with adventure anew
    But reminiscent of times gone by
The moments of stress were but a few.

Though much older, we did not let time fly.
    Closer and closer our emotions made mend,
Old hurts and fears that tears could transcend.

Surrounded by mountains
    Colored brilliantly for the season of fall,
We canoed just once... it was too small.

Rowing a boat each day more fit for four,
    The water moved calm and peaceful.
Then waves sudden and white capped,
    We watched them soar,
Beaching the boat so to have more.

Driving excursions along Route #7
    From Vergennes to Ferrisburgh, and on to Charlotte...
Across on the ferry to Essex, New York
    Meandering south to Ticonderoga,
A little ferry took us back to our Vermont spot.

Walking around Long Point
    Looking out across to the Dean's islands,
We visited long ago cottage haunts.

We cooked hot dogs on a fire between the rocks,
    Eating together once more on that special rocky point.
We marveled at how things seemed the same
    In spite of all the years of change.

Seeing friends of past years,
    Who, too, have grown older.
But in this beautiful place
    Are no less the bolder.

A ride to Camel's Hump near Burrow's cottage
    Brought us treasured thoughts of mountain top heights,
We made, almost, without a fight.

In the evenings each took a turn at cooking,
    Reading books by the fire so bright.
We often played cards with no one looking,
    Listening to music to our hearts delight.

We lounged in pajamas and talked of old times
Events of years gone, but oh, so cherished!
Crying tears of some sadness and often
Laughter from funny behavior,
We sang joyous hymns of our faith and 'our Savior.'

The week's end came too soon, but we did not despair
For one more adventure we would share...
Driving through the mountains, first green and
Then white, from Vermont to New Hampshire; trails at Franconia Notch,
Echo Lake, and the flume so awesome.

Each made a vow we'd do it again.
This fantastic time together,
Of renting a cottage on Lake Champlain,
Once more to claim, Vermont again.

Thank you Sisters!
Lovingly, Margaret
November 1996

And of course we did.

* * *

Row, Row, Row Your Boat…

One of the comical events that occurred during this sister reunion happened on an afternoon when the four sisters decided to take a ride in the rowboat. It was sunny out, but windy with blustery white clouds and the lake wasn't completely calm. In fact it was a bit choppy, but we wanted to be on the water. We all dressed warm since it was October, got into the rowboat with Jeanne at the oars. She and I took turns rowing. We rowed out and around the little point to the bay and across to Long Point.

We went on around the end of Long Point even though it was choppy waters because we thought we would just stick close to shore. We went along the edge south but soon the choppy water now waves two and three feet high, seemed to be getting rougher and so we turned around. Well, we couldn't row against this water.

Harold Stowe was standing by his camp and saw our dilemma. I am sure he was amused. He came down and helped us pull the rowboat out of the water.

We pulled the boat up on the rocks by the *Just A Mere* and next door to *Lotta Water* camp owned by the Stowe family. We asked if we could leave the boat beached there and come back later for it. He agreed this would be the safest thing to do. The sisters sat on the rocks by the beached rowboat deciding what to do next. Barbara and I would walk back to the *Elmwood* and get my car. Jeanne and Bobbie sat up in the little park area across from the *Spindrift* and waited for us to come back and get them.

* * *

This letter from my sister Barbara after the weeks she spent at the sister reunion and with my family in Connecticut and Vermont that year shares her feelings of that time. She left it for me before she departed to go to her home in California.

November 11, 1996

Dear Margaret,

I want to thank you so much for the entire four weeks! It has been wonderful!

I have enjoyed being with you and with your family very much. You've all made me feel so much at home.

The week in Vermont was like a dream I'll never forget!

I especially appreciate Whit being willing to have me here so long. I am glad to have had a chance to know him better. You're both special people!

In this box is a tiny little token of my appreciation.

I don't really have the words or the means to tell you how much it's meant to be here with you. I just hope you could tell how much I enjoyed myself.

Love always,
Barbara

* * *

Good Intentions

Whit and I rented the Kirsch camp, *Elmwood* again in the summer of 1997 with the intention of continuing to do so each summer.

However, Lorna's husband, Mike, a local real estate agent came down to see us one day at camp that summer.

He said to us, "I know you two really want to own a camp since through the years you have looked for one. I think I have just the camp for you." We said, "Where?" Mike's reply, "It isn't part of Long Point, but is only a five minute walk from this camp. It is on the property of the Danyow farm."

Well, we had looked in the past and had even found one on East Road in 1970 that we had considered buying. But at the time we thought it was out of the question. We were married only three years and had two small children. We continued to dream of that day when we might own a camp. I should say, I dreamed, but really didn't think it would happen.

Now in July 1997 Mike was saying to us in so many words, "This may be the time. Why don't you just come and have a look. It is right through those woods, only a five minute walk." I am sure my heart began to thump...to even think that a camp was available in a price range we might afford. Was it possible?

* * *

CAMP OWNERS: 1997

We walked through those woods.

This camp that we were going to look at with Mike was not a part of the land owned by Long Point Association. Instead it was on land adjacent to it. Jack Danyow of the farm off Bay View Road owned this piece of property. I did not know him but I had known his Dad. It was this same farm where my Dad had gone to get night crawlers.

We walked to the woods and through the trees. We had gotten only a few hundred yards into the woods when Mike said, "Look up there." Up in the trees, through a forest of tall cedar, some seventy-five to a hundred feet high, and numerous saplings of many varieties was a camp.

This camp we later learned, named *Lottie* was hardly visible, but Whit and I could see a deck going across the front. The camp had apparently not been used for several years, as the present owner had been ill for sometime. Trees had begun to encroach the deck some leaning precariously on it.

We walked up the narrow stairway, known as the 'common stairway', to the top of a ledge. Honeysuckle bushes and raspberry bushes overgrown from neglect pushed against the back of the little camp. The door to the porch, the only entrance that we could see to get through, was overgrown with these same bushes.

Mike was able to get the lock off and pull the door open. We walked into a screened-in porch that wrapped around to the front. Another door with windows that also had a lock faced a kitchen/eating area. We peered in. There was a well-kept room furnished with vintage porcelain sink, refrigerator, gas stove, table, and chairs. Pots and pans were neatly placed on a shelf. I thought, was this a possibility? I am sure my heart was in my mouth. But surely we would not be able to afford this place?

We continued our inspection by walking out another door from the screened-in porch onto the deck. So many trees encroached it we could not see the view of the lake very well. But there was one. We walked to the end of the camp and peered in the window of the second room, a living room with a Simmons couch and a small chest of drawers. An area rug of the Persian variety covered the floor. The couch we later found opened to a bed. A ladder was seen that went to a little loft.

A side yard at the south end of the property was also full of honeysuckle bushes and high weeds encroaching upon the camp. Was this a camp to seriously consider?

We walked back to our rented camp on Long Point.

We took a couple of days to consider. The price...well, though it seemed fair we knew it would be too much. Whit had just retired from his job with the State of Connecticut and I no longer was working. Even though we still had a mortgage on our home in Connecticut and college loans for our two daughters, we thought maybe we wouldn't have this chance again. So we decided to make an offer.

We couldn't pass it by. We spoke with Mike and made our offer. Incredibly it was accepted.

In some fashion I knew my Mom and Dad, though long gone from this earth had had a hand in this decision.

* * *

The next step was to talk with Jack Danyow and go through the lease for the land. We met at the Danyow farm. Jack, Mike, Whit and I sat in chairs in the picnic area of the farm, once the cow pasture where Dad and I had looked for night crawlers.

The conversation concerning the camp and leased land took place but most of the conversation ended up centered around trains. Whit and Jack found they not only were the same age but they had a common interest in trains. Both belonged to the Rutland Railroad club.

I was encouraged that Whit would find someone of common interests.

* * *

On September 15th, 1997 the closing for camp *Lottie* took place at the lawyers office in Vergennes. The signing took place and we were official owners. I was in absolute ecstasy! Whit and I were really the owners of a camp on leased land in Vermont! Incredible!

Whit and I had six weeks before the end of the vacation season to stay and work on 'our' little two-room camp.

Whit stayed two weeks with me and we began cutting back the bushes and clearing the tree saplings that were growing over the deck. We spoke with Jack about the tree cutting. His main concern was the cedars. "Just don't cut the cedars." And we didn't.

Returning to Connecticut Whit began a part time retirement job at the local hardware store. I stayed on at camp for the remainder of the season with Whit returning on weekends.

I was walking on a cloud. It was all so unbelievable. It was an awesome feeling. We owned a camp in Vermont on the shore of Lake Champlain!

* * *

Those three weeks alone were a joyous time for me as well as a peaceful place for me to do meditation and be on retreat. I had recently left a position of work that had been very stressful for several years and I needed time to just be. This was the perfect place.

During those weeks I had time to reflect. I used Ralph Blum's *Book of Runes* as a tool for meditation as well as the book of *Psalms* from the Old Testament of the Holy Bible. I made some decisions about what I might do when I returned home. I watched beautiful sunsets.

I felt grateful to God for making it possible for Whit and me to buy our little camp.

* * *

We opened our little *Lottie* camp, also known to our family as *Whit's End*, for its first full season, May 1998.

PART IV

FIRST FULL SEASON—CAMP LOTTIE 1998

Whit and I opened our new little camp *Lottie* also known as *Whit's End* and there began the new Vermont stories of the Morse family as camp owners.

Several procedures have to take place in order to open camp. The electricity has to be turned on. This means a call several days ahead to the Green Mountain Power Company. The telephone has to get turned on too, meaning another phone call from Connecticut to the telephone company in Vermont.

The water comes from the lake and is pumped through pipes into the camp. The pump has to get turned on. We put antifreeze into the drains to keep pipes from freezing over the winter. Once we get to camp each season the antifreeze has to be flushed out. Windows are opened and the camp aired out. We do a thorough vacuuming of the whole place before making up beds and putting out towels etc.

We don't drink the water from the lake so we bring water from home upon arrival. Once we are settled into camp drinking water can be gotten from a common well in Vergennes, groceries purchased and food shelves stocked.

That first season we felt overwhelmed by all the procedures but over these several years we have become adapt.

* * *

A Place of Retreat

In the living room/bedroom of the camp is a poster. It was left hanging on the wall by Patricia Starr the former owner. It is a picture of a wood with a poem by Ralph Waldo Emerson.

> Think me not unkind and rude,
> that I walk alone in grove and glen.
> I go to the God of the wood
> to fetch His word to men.

I had opportunity in this first full summer season to use this beautiful hideaway as a place of retreat for several weeks and use it also for clients I had in my new vocation of giving spiritual direction. Whit and I enjoyed bringing friends as well. The poem by Mr. Emerson was a perfect statement of what we wanted our camp *Lottie* to be.

There would be no television or VCR. I really didn't want a telephone either and had gone without one the first month that I stayed alone in 1997. However, through a group family decision, a telephone was put in and eventually a message machine for family and clients use.

* * *

Client Experience

The first opportunity I had for making a retreat was with Rose (This name has been changed as a matter of confidentiality). We came to the camp and spent four days in a semi-silent retreat. We used the *Book of Runes* by Ralph Blum, drawing a rune each morning to set a focus for our day. I set up meditative readings for both of us to work on in a silent atmosphere each morning. In the afternoon we might do one or several relaxing activities. These would include walking, canoeing, reading out on the deck, etc.

In the evening we shared what we had learned while sitting on the deck or porch to watch a splendid sunset.

It was my joy to cook and serve each meal.

This semi-retreat with Rose is an example of the several experiences I was able to provide for clients through that summer and it has been Whit's and my blessing to share our camp in this way.

* * *

Getting Settled

During my first weeks at Camp Lottie I was fortunate to have my long-time friend Lorna come and help me get settled in.

One day we went to Burlington to Recycle North to buy a used washing machine, and a rollaway bed for $2.00. We did some necessary errands on the way, stopping at the Titus Insurance Company in Shelburne to see about insurance for my canoe. We went to the boat exchange to look at used aluminum boats and motors for future reference. On the way home we went to lunch at Burdocks Country Kitchen in Ferrisburgh and then went to Vergennes for groceries and water.

* * *

A Bird Sanctuary

In mid-May my friend Carolyn came for several days.

Carolyn is a bird watcher and was able to share her knowledge about a variety of birds. She would sit on the deck and listen. Then she would tell me what bird she was hearing. I was in awe. I came to know that this little wood is in actuality a wonderful bird sanctuary.

* * *

Through the summer pileated red-head woodpeckers, grouse, Baltimore orioles, robins, cardinals, blue jays, mourning doves, hawks, osprey, golden finch, several different warblers, and even a couple of eagles were seen. I began a bird journal to keep track of each bird I saw or heard and purchased a couple of bird books.

* * *

Reconnecting With An Old Friend

At the end of May I spent a special four days with an old high school friend, Jackie, who I had not seen in thirty-eight years. We had reconnected by mail during the winter as she now lives in Wells River, Vermont in the region known as Northeast Kingdom.

I sent her directions to get to my camp. On the day she was to arrive I decided I would walk out to Greenbush Road to meet her. She would have to pass me so I figured I could wave her down. But that was not to be.

I walked all the way out to Greenbush Road and then turned around. As I walked past the railroad crossing coming back a turquoise van passed me. Jackie had told me what kind of car to look for. I knew this van had to be her. As I started to wave the van stopped and pulled into a driveway. I assumed Jackie had seen me and kept walking. But I was wrong. The van backed up out of the driveway and continued on down the road. I began to run and wave my arm, yelling "Stop. Jackie, stop." But of course to no avail as she could not see or hear me.

I continued on and when I got back to the camp fifteen minutes later she was at the camp standing on the deck taking in the view of the lake.

We spent our first day together catching up on our lives, and then the next three days in a semi-retreat, using the runes to focus our day and spending the morning in meditation and silence. We would share at lunch and in the afternoon we walked, canoed, or sat on the deck reading. This old/new friend is a very faithful Christian, and a delightful free spirited woman.

* * *

A New Vermont Connection

On a Thursday in May I took a drive to Colchester, Vermont to visit Betty Cross, a sweet, gentle woman that I had been introduced to through her sister, June.

June Austin is the Patient Counselor at the IAT Centre, a cancer clinic in the Bahamas where my daughter Torrey had been a patient and continues to return for yearly tune-ups. This clinic offers a treatment that augments the immune system of the cancer patient so that he/she can fight his or her own disease.

Betty is a patient also at this clinic and I was pleased to have the opportunity to meet this delightful, sincere woman. Betty and I went to Zachary's Pizza house and had lunch and visited over a glass of wine. I promised to bring Torrey back with me to meet her.

* * *

A Lake Storm

Twice in two weeks during my time alone at camp the wind and rain came across the lake into our little cedar wood. The power went out both times and I had to use candles in the evenings for light.

I found it exciting to watch a storm come across the lake toward the Vermont shore.

During one such storm I stood on the deck and watched the wind build up and the rain begin on the lake. I watched the tall cedars and birch begin to slowly sway back and forth. Then the wind gusts moved them faster and I began to feel and hear the beginning of the rain in the wood.

A blue jay nest slowly moved back and forth but was safe under the eve of a nearby camp. A robin's nest in a cedar close by was rocked pretty vigorously but did not fall out. A large branch from a cedar tree was blown back and forth and finally did break off, falling to the ground. Soon the rain came in large pelts onto the deck.

I quickly grabbed the hanging petunia plant off the deck and stepped inside our screened-in porch. I continued to watch the wind and rain.

I gathered candles and put batteries into my radio for emergency power outage and readied myself for the evening. I have a gas stove so I knew I could have hot tea. I had a phone too, but wasn't worried if it went out. I made up my bed on the sofa and got my book to read.

I took a blanket and tacked it over the doorway from the living room to the kitchen to keep my little area cozy.

The power did go out but I had my candles lit and my hot tea ready. Because the refrigerator was not on I knew things would begin to thaw. In the little freezer was some ice cream. There was only one solution for it and that was for me to eat it. And so I did.

About two hours later the power came back on. I turned on my little oil heater and soon I was toasty warm. Reading until eleven p.m. and then receiving two phone calls I went to sleep feeling content and blessed.

* * *

Housekeeping of the Property

Whit came for several days at the beginning of June. We worked on the property. He cut down three trees that were encroaching the deck and built a rock wall for an azalea bush in the rock garden. I cleaned inside the camp and then carried the cut logs from the bottom of the hill to the car. We have a wood stove in Connecticut so the wood came in handy.

* * *

Finding A Church

On that same weekend I went to church with Mary Gordon and her Mom, Adele, at the Trinity Episcopal Church, Shelburne, Vermont. I go to an Episcopal Church in Connecticut so I was pleased to find someone else to attend church with me.

Mary's mom is a fascinating eighty-eight year old adopted Vermonter, originally coming to Vermont from Austria via Connecticut. She at one time owned and lived during the summers in a cabin on the side of Camel's Hump, my favorite mountain.

I attended this beautiful little brownstone church for three months.

* * *

Car Episode

That same Sunday afternoon Whit and I had what could have been a long and tiresome ordeal. After a light lunch we started out for Montpelier, the capital of Vermont to go visit our friends, Mike and Cindy Fessel, who live in Middlesex. We went in my 1986 Honda Accord driving across country through Hinesburg and Williston before getting on I89. Twenty miles down I89 my Honda started acting strange. It finally began slowing down and I had to pull over to the side of the road and park.

I don't have a car phone so we put the emergency flashing lights on and waited for a Vermont State trooper. This first wait was about forty-five minutes to an hour.

When the trooper finally appeared he was very pleasant but in a hurry to get to another emergency on up the road. He stopped just long enough to tell us that he would call for a tow truck.

The second wait was another hour for the tow truck from Richmond, Vermont. The driver put my car on the flat bed and then informed us that he didn't have room for both of us because he had his girlfriend with him. He called for a taxi.

We were not happy about this situation since we now would have to pay for both a tow truck and a taxi and it was beginning to drizzle light rain. We had to stand in the rain while waiting for the taxi.

When the taxi came I went with it and Whit went with the tow truck driver and girlfriend. I used the taxi driver's phone to call our friends, Lorna and Mike, to see if one of them could come pick us up in Shelburne at the Automaster. This is where we were being taken. Lorna very kindly agreed.

While Whit and I were waiting for the State trooper, the tow truck and the taxi we might have gotten terribly irritated at each other and at them. I know that accusations about the car might have occurred, but they did not. Fortunately I believe we have both learned that it would do no good for either of us to be impatient. Of course we did not want to deal with the car breaking down, or any of the situation with the tow truck or taxi but we had no choice. Therefore, we chose not to become impatient and irritated at the situation. We were actually telling stories of similar occasions and laughing about this present situation during the wait. I was glad Whit had been with me.

* * *

Continued Car Aggravation

The next day Whit had to return to Connecticut so I had to call the car dealer and see what was being done with my Honda. I knew I had to go home to Connecticut too the following weekend so I would need the car. They ended up having my car for nearly the whole week. I picked it up on Friday and drove home on Saturday.

I made it all the way home, but on Saturday the car died on me again. I had my local garage person look at it and he readjusted the carburetor that the Automaster garage people had supposedly cleaned.

I drove back to Vermont the next week and had just pulled into the camp parking area when the car stalled again. I was able to get it started and took it to the Automaster once more.

I had a friend with me that day, a former stock car driver, who was visiting with his wife. He was great. When I was told by this garage that I should put in a new gas tank John said, 'No thank you.' We left. John's recommendation was to get some dry gas and put it in the tank and fill up with high test. I did this and guess what? My car has run smoothly for three years. Every once in a while I put in dry gas and I continue to use high test.

* * *

John and Miriam

Our friends John and Miriam had come to go kayaking. They marveled at this little camp in the cedar wood overlooking Lake Champlain.

Miriam reminded me of my sister, Jeanne, in her keen intelligence and joyous spirit. She was obviously a person who enjoyed the outdoors and spoke of her camping experience. When I showed Miriam the bed on the porch she immediately said, "I would like to sleep there." And this is where Jeanne sleeps when she comes to visit.

The first evening I cooked a pasta meal with a vegetable sautéed mixture of zucchini, broccoli, green peppers and onions that I blended with a tomato sauce. A side salad and bread were included.

John and I had been involved in a community organization for several years and so following the meal we sat around the table and caught up on that group and conversed about such topics as our belief in the 'higher power', reincarnation, attitude for living in today's world, etc.

It was after nine p.m. when we finally got up and cleared the table. Miriam washed the dishes and I dried. We had had a long day so we all retired to our beds to read.

In the morning I had my cup of coffee on the deck and did my daily meditation, drawing a 'rune,' reading from the *Book of Runes* and focusing on its message. I read some scripture from the Psalms and did some writing.

When John and Miriam got up they had breakfast with me and then set about getting ready for a day of kayaking on the lake.

* * *

A Friend's Visit

My friend Helen from Connecticut came to stay for several days in June. This would be her vacation so I wanted the time to go well for her.

We started our day by picking a rune and reading the meditation for it. And we would walk each morning. Then we would just do what ever we felt like whether it be canoeing, reading, taking a drive, etc.

I did the cooking most nights but Helen enjoyed cooking too so she did a couple of times. One evening she made a delicious stir-fry of vegetables that she put on spaghetti with sauce. She served it with garlic bread and a glass of wine. Scrumptious! We sat and watched one of Vermont's spectacular sunsets to end our evening.

* * *

A Geese Story

I got up to go walking one morning in June with another new friend, Elaine. It was about 7:20 a.m.. when I heard quacking sounds. I looked out over the deck at the lake and saw a flock of geese were coming in for a landing in our little Pleasant Bay. I thought no more about it and poured my coffee. Then I heard more quacking and what was deep throated grunting. I went out on the deck to see, but I could only hear splashing sounds and the grunting sounds.

It was time for the walk with Elaine. So I called and said "I am leaving now, where shall we meet?" She wanted to postpone the walk for half an hour.

Well, she had given me a gift! I could now go down to our neighbor's deck and look to see what was going on with the geese. I was curious to see what was happening.

In the water were three sets of goslings, at various growth stages and five adult females. They were feeding close to the shore. Two males, in position like 'point guards,' swam to one side. Out farther were five more adult males swimming and occasionally grunting toward the goslings and females. Out about twenty feet or so from them were another seventeen geese waiting and feeding. I found it fascinating to see the whole flock being a part of the feeding of the baby goslings. I thought of community and its purpose. These geese all had their various functions.

About ten minutes or so later an authoritative honk went out and the whole flock began to move.

The goslings and females moved out away from the shore and back toward the waiting geese. The two 'point guards' moved over to where they had been and it was if they were checking to see that all were on the move. Several males (I think) moved in toward the two adult 'point guards.' At first I though maybe these two weren't guards but intruders because the five males moved toward them, grunting and the two came fast toward them with heads down and pointing straight out. Several deep-throated sounds were made between the two groups of two and five adults. They all began moving out to the open bay where the twenty-two goslings and adults, I think females, had gone. The rest of the flock had moved in behind them. The whole flock slowly moved along the shore continuing to feed before they flew away. This whole scenario was an awesome sight. One I had never witnessed and now felt privileged to see.

* * *

A Vermont Excursion and History Lesson

One beautiful June day Lorna picked me up and we drove to Monkton to the Barnebus Barnard cemetery. Lorna was the caretaker at the time and saw to the property up keep, etc. We walked around and I enjoyed reading the various names and epitaphs on the gravestones.

She told me a little of her family history. I saw a gravestone with the name Aloha Dean. This is the name of one of her sisters. The story is that a Native American woman named Aloha had saved the great, great, great grandfather of Lorna's from death. When this man had married he named his daughter after this Native American woman. The original Aloha's sister was Malia. Both of these names were chosen by Lorna's father to name her two older sisters.

It seems that when Lorna was being born her dad, Leon Dean, was reading the book *Lorna Doone* to the two sisters. Hence the new baby was given the name Lorna.

* * *

Lorna and I continued on to other cemeteries. We went to Bristol and put flowers on her Mom and Dad's graves. Many of the Dean family relatives are buried there. Lorna's Dad died in 1982 at age 92 and her Mom in 1996 at age 101.

* * *

A Book Connection

After our cemetery exploring we went to check out Deerleap Books, a bookstore in Bristol and talked with the owner.

I had written my first book, *Choices A Journey of Faith—Torrey's Miracle,* about my daughter, Torrey, her walk with cancer and her healing through an alternative treatment. I hoped to make arrangements for a book event and have some of my books sold there. The book would come in to the selling market in 1999 and I was trying to make connections ahead.

Lorna and I ate lunch at a local deli.

* * *

Canoeing

Later that same day when I had returned to camp I decided to go for a canoe ride. I went for a walk first and saw my friend, Mary Gordon, who was out riding her bike. I asked her to go in the canoe with me. We went and picked up the paddles and life preservers at the camp and went down to the beach for the canoe.

We paddled around to the main bay and across to the Dean's Islands. We both expressed our joy at being on this awesome lake. We paddled along the edge of the lakeshore by the ledges back into Pleasant Bay and by what is known as 'turtle rock.' We saw several turtles sunbathing on the ledge and several ducks with their goslings.

* * *

A Family Visit with the Dog

It is always a joy when any of the family visit camp. Our daughter, Jessica, and her husband, Dan, came to visit for a weekend with their puppy, a corgi, named Quigley. They brought Whit with them as a surprise. I wasn't expecting him until the next week.

It rained the whole weekend. This was too bad for Whit because he had projects he wanted to do. Also this was Jessica and Dan's first visit so it would put a cramp into the time.

However, we made the best of it and during a respite from the rain we took them on a walk around Long Point. Quigley liked the walk and even stuck one paw into the water along the edge. He wasn't sure he wanted to go in the water but did venture a paw and then two.

During the rain Saturday afternoon we played one of our favorite card games, Canasta.

In the evening while the rain was letting up, Whit cooked steaks on the grill for dinner. We then settled in to read. I have an assortment of novels and non-fiction available for all visitors.

We took another walk in the rain early Sunday morning and then went to Burdick's country kitchen restaurant for breakfast before they all headed back to Connecticut.

* * *

Camp Catch-up

I spent the next three hours cleaning the camp. I made signs for starting the gas stove, how to shut the refrigerator door, where parking a car was acceptable, and the use of the toilet facilities, etc.

* * *

More Friends

Guilford friends, Gail and Eugene O'Leary came to visit one weekend bringing with them two young men visiting from Spain and the daughter of their neighbors who were away. Gail and Eugene wanted to share another part of the country with these two young men besides Connecticut so they came to Vermont.

Eugene and I wanted to give them a canoe experience, but the water was too choppy and they did not know how to paddle a canoe. I offered to take them all to my friend Elaine's to swim but only Gail went with me. We took a ride down to the Dead Creek bird refuge and a ride up into the mountains over Appalachian Gap.

* * *

July 4th - A Mouse Experience

When I had returned to camp after a brief trip to Connecticut one weekend I found little pieces of Kleenex on the floor in the living room. I just picked them up and didn't think anything about it. A week later Whit and I invited our friends Cindy and Mike for a July 4th picnic at the camp.

The holiday turned out to be a rainy day so when they arrived we sat on the screened in porch. Whit brought the Weber grill in to the porch for doing the cooking. We sat and had a glass of wine and some snacks. I had made my homemade five baked beans and they were reheating in the gas oven.

While the four of us chatted, there seemed to be a funny smell, a rather strange odor beginning to permeate our nostrils. It was slight but soon seemed to penetrate the air. We had eaten fish the night before. Perhaps it was left over drippings in the oven. Yet, somehow this smell was different.

An hour later this funny odor was becoming really sickening. All of us were getting a queasy feeling from the dead sweet odor. I went and opened the oven to look. The odor was definitely coming from the oven. It was now disgustingly strong. On a closer inspection I looked where there is a broiler pan under the oven. There in the drip catching space of the broiler oven was a little dead body. It was a small field mouse. And there was also a burned nest. Now I knew how the Kleenex pieces had gotten on the floor previously. The field mouse had made a nest. It was now charcoal. I didn't even want to think about any little babies.

I don't know if the gas had killed this little mouse when I turned it on or the heat but now we had to get rid of her and the burned to a crisp nest.

Of course no one wanted to touch it. But Mike took on the task. He took two potholders that he put brown paper bags on and picked up the broiler pan that I had already removed from the oven. He carried it out on to the deck in the rain and proceeded to shake it over the rail of the deck. However, the burned to a crisp mouse didn't come off. Mike then reached out to pull it off. He shouted out and danced up and down. A leg had come off and was stuck to the bag he had on his hand. Whit, Cindy and I were making disgusting noises and laughing at him and the whole situation. Mike finally loosened it and cleaned off the broiling pan.

The beans that I had cooked in the oven we decided not to eat. I imagine they would have been okay. They had a lid on them. But the smell from the burned mouse had penetrated the camp and the thought of the beans having cooked in the same oven...well, we just couldn't eat them. I set the pot of beans out on the deck away from us.

We opened all the windows to air out the camp and continued on with the cooking of our hamburgers on the grill.

The mouse subject came up several times during dinner. We thought it best not to tell any of the guests coming to visit for the next few weeks.

Upon inspection the next day after the incident Whit found a place under the screen door that seemed large enough for a small mouse to get in. He found a piece of wood to nail over the hole. We haven't had any mice since.

* * *

A Dog named Remington and the Ice Cream Cone

Whit and I drove to Vergennes one afternoon to get water at the common water fount in the park. There was a band concert taking place so we decided to stay and listen. We were in time to hear the last number, The Star Spangled Banner. We then decided to go get ice cream at the Main Street ice cream place where they offer a large variety of hard and soft ice cream.

We bought our cones and sat down at a picnic bench to eat them. While we were enjoying the ice cream we noticed a big German Shepard who was interested in the people eating their ice cream cones.

One of the sales clerks, a young teenage girl, saw the dog and leaned out the window. She said, "Here Remington." In her hand she had a cone filled with Vanilla ice cream. At first the dog didn't take notice, but when she said his name again, "Remington," he walked over to the window. He jumped up and put both paws on the counter in front of the window. The girl put the cone out the window and the dog took it in his mouth. He then went over to a shady spot and proceeded to eat his ice cream cone. All the customers were extremely entertained.

* * *

Train Country

Whit and his friend, Don, arrived Saturday from Connecticut about 4 p.m. after meandering up through Vermont following the train tracks of the Rutland Railroad across the state. Both are model train buffs and also enjoy the real thing, especially Don.

They spent the next day after they got to camp driving north above Burlington to South Hero, North Hero and the islands. They went across the causeway into New York to Rouses Point and then up into Canada looking for a specific train. It sounded like they had quite an adventurous excursion.

* * *

A Borrowed Motorboat - The Mirrorcraft

In that first season at our camp I looked for a small motorboat that I might buy and use on the lake. I didn't know whether I wanted a used or a new one.

On a morning in July after my morning walk with friends, Elaine Saltus and Mary Gordon, I met another woman on Long Point, Pat Stacey. Elaine introduced us. She owned a small fourteen-foot Mirrorcraft boat that she was considering selling. It had a fifteen horsepower motor on it and a side console.

After some conversation Pat took me out in the little boat, showed me the basics of running it, told me about the gas and oil mixing, and then let me take it out alone.

Pat's neighbor, Wendell Northrup from Rutland, Vermont and owner of the camp *Windleblow*, helped us launch the boat.

* * *

Wendell Northrup

I had known Wendell when I was a teenager near the end of 1950's. It was interesting to meet this man now in his 70's whom I had known so long ago.

His family had been a part of Long Point since the late 1800s and the camp *Windleblow* that he owned was one of the original camps built by the bay. Wendell and his wife, Betty were summer residents of many years.

It was Wendell's aunt, Bertha Stillson Ranger who wrote her own reminisces of the area, *Long Point Memories* in 1980. This unpublished manuscript shares history of Long Point previous to when my parents and family first arrived.

* * *

The First Ride

As Pat and I went out on that first ride through the bay and around the Dean's islands I felt such great joy! We rode across to Gardiner's Island and back around Long Point. I was ecstatic.

Pat and I agreed that I would use the boat through the remaining weeks of July and August with the possible option to buy.

I loved using this little craft and giving rides to family and friends. I had a canoe but having this little motorboat was such a delight for me.

I did not go out far onto the broad lake because it had been many years since I had been on this lake and run a boat. I knew that a storm could/would come up very quickly.

* * *

A Place of Harbor

The water level of the lake was high that summer because of all the rain due to El Nino. The beach area where I might have pulled the boat up was under water. Fortunately one of our new friends, Bob Gordon let me put our canoe on his dock and let me moor the motorboat there for a week or so. He then got permission from another camp owner to use her dock. Because of the rain I had to bail the boat many times before using it.

* * *

My First Passenger

The first person I gave a ride to was Mary Gordon. The marvelous delight of being on the lake and seeing the mountains from that perspective and driving the boat was awesome. I couldn't believe I really had use of a motorboat. We were not out too long, but when we came into the Gordon's dock her Mom was there. So we asked her to go and we went out for a brief ride.

Adele, then eighty-eight relished in this ride as much as we did. The little child within each of us was right at the surface of enjoyment.

* * *

Rides With My Family

When Whit and our two daughters visited we took rides in the boat too. It was especially fun when Jessica and Dan brought their dog, Quigley with us in the boat. On one occasion the water was a little rough and the waves splashed on all of us, soaking us. The puppy wasn't sure what to make of it.

Torrey and I got one long ride in before the end of the summer.

Figure 6 Whitney, Mike and Lorna Brown, Torrey Morse on the Charlotte Ferry; Mom (Margaret Morse) and Torrey in the Mirrorcraft, 1998.

* * *

I made the decision at the end of the summer not to buy the boat, but oh what fun while I had it! I have been ever grateful to my friend, Pat for allowing me to use her little Mirrorcraft.

Another two years would go by before I did purchase a boat.

* * *

A Sailing Adventure

About the same time I first went out in the motorboat I also went for a sail. I am not oriented toward sailing. I don't like to be out of control. However, when my friend, Mary Gordon, asked me I said, "Yes." I told her I had not been on a sailboat of any kind in thirty-three years. She had a little sunfish. She said, "No, problem."

We took two life preservers and went down to where the sunfish was. We pushed it out into the lake. I don't know anything so I sit with my preserver on in the forward part of the little boat. She says, "Just lean when needed and duck when you need too."

We make it out into Pleasant Bay. Mary notices that one of the ropes is not tied where it should be. There isn't much wind to speak of. She says, "Hold on to the sail, and I'll fix this..." "Okay, I've got it." I reply.

No sooner had I said this and the boat begins to tip to the right. We fall into the lake. I wished I had a video camera because the look of surprise on Mary's face and I am sure mine, was probably priceless.

We were not hurt. We were not in a situation of life or death, and the water was not too cold, but we were not going to be able to turn the little sailboat back over to its right side. The sail was hanging straight down and was weighty. We decided to push the boat closer to shore, though we knew we had to be very careful of the ledges because of the sail hanging down. It wouldn't do to have them get torn.

Mary kept saying, "Fifteen years and this never happened."

I was feeling guilty. Perhaps being a novice, I had leaned the wrong way, etc. She kept repeating to me, "Are you all right?" I was fine and I didn't mind being in the water. I was not afraid.

We later noted that both of us had had similar thoughts about Adele. "What if Mary's mom sees us?" Mary's mother would be upset and worried if she had seen us. She usually takes a nap during the afternoon so I think we both hoped she was napping. What about Bob? What would he do? He was out mowing so he probably had not seen.

Fortunately, a Vermont police boat from Troop A appeared. They were out patrolling the waters. I felt happy about their arrival, as I knew we couldn't right the boat. And they affirmed this fact. If we had gone closer to shore than we were we might have mutilated the sail on the rocky ledges. I knew Mary felt embarrassed. I didn't think she should, as I thought it was my fault.

However, these things happen and we were taking a swim instead of a sail. The water was not too cold and we were finally able to laugh and let our stress out and our humiliation.

The Vermont police boat manned by Auxiliary Trooper Erik Lavallee and his dad, Dutch Lavallee, out of East Middlebury had come to our rescue. They helped us aboard their motor craft and called the Point Bay marina.

Two young men from Point Bay came with a barge craft. They were able to upright the little sailboat without any damage to it. We boarded this craft and they gave us a ride back to Mary's dock while towing the little boat.

When we got to Mary's her Mom walked down to the dock and wanted to know who had brought us home. She had not seen us turn over, much to our relief. Though embarrassing and humiliating this was a funny adventure to remember.

* * *

A Friends Visit

My dear friend Kasha and husband, Edwin came for two days. It was such a delight to share our little retreat with them. I took them out to Long Point sharing the panoramic views of Lake Champlain as well as telling them stories of my childhood years. We took a drive up into the Green mountains and relished in the wonder of God's magnificent creation.

* * *

Mozart Festival

Every July the Vermont Symphony presents the Mozart Festival series. The symphony plays concerts in various places throughout the state, some outside along the shore of Lake Champlain. I went to several of these concerts during that first year with some of my Vermont friends. We would take a blanket, chairs, and a picnic to eat while listening to the concert offered by the symphony and/or guest musicians.

* * *

A Visit With Torrey

In August Whit and I had the pleasure of having our daughter, Torrey, come spend time with us. She had a week between an old job with JOB Core of Connecticut and beginning a new one with the State of Connecticut. She enjoyed walking with me in the morning, sitting on the deck to read, going out in the little Mirrorcraft with us and taking the ferry from Charlotte with us across the lake to The Old Dock House, one of our favorite restaurants in Essex, New York.

* * *

A Vermont Surprise Birthday

On August 17, 1998 Whit turned sixty years old. He had asked me not to have a party for him as I had when he retired in 1997. This had been in Connecticut. So I said I wouldn't.

On August 8th Whit came for one of his weekend visits. I had called up all the people we had met this first year and a half as camp owners. I invited Mary and Bob Gordon, Elaine and Urban Saltus from Long Point; Ron and Alice Gabriel our new neighbors; Jack and Lee Danyow from the farm; Lorna and Mike our long time Vermont friends. My sister, Jeanne, from Illinois was visiting us as well as our children: Torrey, Jessica and husband, Dan.

We had a 60th Birthday Party surprise! All the guests brought a hot dish to share and we cooked hot dogs, hamburgers on the grill and served wine, beer and soft drinks.

When Whit, a little bit annoyed, said, "I thought you weren't going to throw a party." I responded. "I didn't have one in Connecticut, but this was a great way to get our new friends together."

It was great fun to watch the guests get to know one another. Mary and Alice had played tennis together twenty years previously and now were meeting again.

For some reason I had not thought of getting a cake and toward the end of the evening Lorna and Mike took Torrey with them to Vergennes to purchase a cake and buy ice cream for all to enjoy.

Everyone liked the festivities of the day, even Whitney!

* * *

THE BERGER SISTER REUNION

Swimming

When my sisters arrived for their reunion week with me at our new Camp Lottie the water was still high and covered the beach area.

On the piece of land called the 'common ground' shared by the lease owners there is a cliff by the water. This is where we went swimming. A rope tied to a cedar tree went down into the water. It was easy getting in, because you would either jump or dive. But getting out through the use of this rope was not so easy for four women whose ages were in the 50's and 60's.

More often than not we would go to Kingsland Bay State Park to swim where there was a big cement dock, steps and small beach.

Once the French School for girls this piece of land became a state park in 1974.

Besides having a place to swim at this lovely park there are walking trails that go along the edge of the water around a peninsula of land known as MacDonough Point. There are boats for rowing and canoes to rent.

Many people use the park for a variety of reasons, one being weddings and receptions and the Vermont State Symphony uses the park for a couple of the concerts during the July-Vermont Mozart series.

* * *

The Berger Sister Excursions

While the sisters were visiting we had several happy adventures out on the lake in the borrowed motorboat. We motored across our little bay and around the end of Long Point between 'the point' and 'the rocks,' along the cliff, across to Gardiner's Island and to Kingsland Bay, places we had gone as children.

We would motor over to and around the Dean's Islands and reminisce about those fun-filled days when we vacationed on this beautiful lake so many years ago.

One day we packed a picnic lunch and motored over behind Gardiner's Island just as I remember the L'Hommedieus doing. We let the boat drift and ate our lunch sitting there in Hawkins Bay. We all felt as if we were living a dream.

My sister, Jeanne, and I went out with Pat to fish too.

* * *

Trip to Kingsland Bay—Singing Debut

One of our trips to Kingsland Bay was on a gloriously sunny, windy day. The water was choppy so we couldn't take the little motorboat. Instead we drove. It is only about fifteen minutes by car.

We wore our swim suits, took our blankets, beach towels, books, writing materials and, of course, a delicious picnic lunch. We had bought sandwiches from Hanlon's market to go with fruit and cheese, cold drinks and cookies.

My sisters and I have always liked to sing. As young adults the older three sang with another woman as a quartet often providing the music for the Sunday evening service for my Dad's church. As I got older I joined them but only for a short period of time.

Now when we are together we just automatically enjoy singing our old favorite hymns and music from the 40's and 50's.

This particular day while the four of us were swimming off the cement dock area, we were singing old favorite hymns and doing our harmonizing. A wedding had already taken place on the grounds of the park and a reception was taking place in one of the buildings.

While my sisters and I were singing a little girl, my guess her age would be five or six, came down onto the dock. She looked out at us and said, "Would you sing *'Jesus Loves Me'*?"

And so we did, in four parts. Barbara would sing the soprano, Bobbie and I the alto and sometimes split this up, and Jeanne, tenor. Soon we were getting requests for other hymns from the wedding guests. We didn't mind the requests because we like to sing. However, we stayed in the water to do them since we were in our swimming suits.

* * *

Another Surprise Birthday

Jeanne turned sixty-two years old on August 22nd while the four sisters were together. We had to celebrate. We began her day by singing '*Happy Birthday'* to her at breakfast and giving presents and cards. We spent another fantastic day at Kingsland Bay State Park.

In the evening we took her to dinner at another of our favorite Vermont restaurants the Dog Team Tavern in Middlebury.

Our parents had always gone to the Dog Team Tavern for their anniversary on August 6th each year that we vacationed in Vermont.

* * *

A Favorite Place to Eat

I introduced my sisters to The Old Dock House restaurant in Essex, NY too. We drove to the ferry in Charlotte, about twenty minutes, parked and walked on the ferry to ride across the lake. We each had a wonderful meal at the restaurant. But more than that it was the ride across Lake Champlain that we loved. It was the joy of being on the water, watching the waves, looking at the grand view of the Adirondacks of New York, and the Green Mountains of Vermont that was cherished.

* * *

Northeast Kingdom Excursion

While the sisters visited we had a grand drive and different adventure up in the Northeast Kingdom. I had early on during the summer noticed a singing event in the *Vermont Events* catalog.

The Old West Church, Calais, VT was holding an Evening Vespers and hymn sing each Sunday evening through the month of August. A potluck supper would also be held. Calais is northeast of Montpelier and about a good hour and a half from our camp on the lake. We decided to go the night of August 23rd. I called to see if we might attend and that I would bring baked beans as a contribution for the potluck supper.

We left the lake and the camp in mid-afternoon on an overcast and cool day. We drove east across the Hinesburg road from Charlotte. We drove to Richmond, Vermont first because we wanted to visit the Round Church built in 1823. After a brief tour there and hearing the history of its founding, we drove on. We chose not to go by I 89 but on route #2. We wanted to view the scenery at a slower pace and see Vermont towns.

We arrived in Montpelier following directions to the Old West Church in Calais by going up County Road, north. We stopped at the Morse Farm (no relation to our Morse's) to take a break and buy some ginger cookers. We then journeyed past the Kent Tavern, an historic site near the church, arriving fifteen minutes before the Evening Vespers.

The Evening Vespers included a musical selection by a six-person choir singing beautifully *'A Balm in Gilead'* as well as a two other selections. The Rev. Dr. Wayne R. Whitlock president of the Old West Church Historical Association led the service and meeting that followed. The Rev. Dr. Robert Sanders, Camp Chaplain Emeritus, Princeton Seminary was the meditation speaker. My sisters and I were interested that both of these gentlemen had attended Princeton Seminary where our Dad had gone. Dr. Sander's meditation was on the Third Millennium.

The hymn sing following the service was fun, singing those grand old hymns of our faith. However, in my sister's and my opinion the hymn sing was too short. We have always liked singing and especially when we are together. Several people had noticed that we were harmonizing and asked if we would sing a hymn for them. We did this later during the potluck supper outside, singing *'I Come to the Garden Alone.'*

My sisters and I, of course, entertained conversation about our family and parents with the two Reverends and others during the potluck.

We met another visiting couple from New Jersey vacationing in Bethel, Vermont.

* * *

Howard Frank Mosher

Howard Frank Mosher is a Vermont author who writes about Vermont, primarily the Northeast Kingdom. I have three of his books at the camp for visitors to read: *A Stranger In the Kingdom, Northern Borders,* and *A River Runs North.*

While My Sisters were visiting we went to see the movie that had just been produced locally of *A Stranger In the Kingdom* at the Vergennes Opera House. It was especially fun to see the locals picking out people they knew who were in the movie.

* * *

Summary of Berger Reunion

While we were together my sisters and I relished every moment. We walked, talked, swam, took rides in the borrowed boat, took drives into the mountains, played cards, in particular Canasta and went out to eat on several evenings.

We memorized the poem from the poster on my living room wall at camp by Ralph Waldo Emerson and we also learned a short poem by Leo Tolstoy that we said each night. One of my college roommates had taught it to me thirty-six years ago.

Good Night, Good Night,
Far flies the light.
But, still God's love
Shall flame above,
Making all bright.
Good Night, Good Night.

* * *

Excursion with Barbara to Connecticut

In September Jeanne and Bobbie, two of the sisters went back to their homes Barbara stayed for another two weeks and we took time to drive down to

Connecticut to visit with my two daughters, Torrey, Jessica and her husband Dan. Whit was home too.

We enjoyed a wonderful week seeing various parts of Connecticut: the Thimble Islands in Long Island Sound; Gillette Castle in Chester, Connecticut; the Henry Whitfield House and Griswold House in Guilford, and of course visiting with the family.

* * *

Return Trip to Vermont

On the Saturday after Labor Day weekend Barbara and I got up at 4 a.m. to begin our journey north to Vermont. We drove the usual route up I91 through Connecticut and Massachusetts and into Vermont as far as Rockingham just past Bellows Falls, Vermont. It had begun to rain but we did not mind. We turned west onto Hwy.103 past the Country Store and through Chester and Ludlow. At Ludlow we decided not to continue across 103 to Rutland, but to turn north up Route 100.

We drove north through President Coolidge country and the cheese factory, through Hancock (Robert Frost country) and on to Warren.

We decided to drive west across the mountain through Lincoln Gap and the village of Lincoln to Bristol.

We were searching for my Dad's favorite trout fishing spot. The road across the mountain was open but there was a sign "Road Closed drive at your own risk." Apparently the road was washed out in a lot of places from all the summer rainstorms. We decided to go ahead.

Even though it was rainy we could see. We drove up and over the mountain along the New Haven River and through the quaint little village of Lincoln. We kept looking for that fishing spot. There were so many beautiful scenic spots along the river. We would see a place and both say, "There it is." But no, the spots we saw were not the place, so we would drive on.

Just as we came down the last slope going into Bristol, Barbara yells, "This is it." And so it was. We parked along the side of the road and walked down an embankment and over near the river that was to our left.

We saw the water falls where once was the viaduct that our dad had crossed over to fish from the other side. The remnants of the viaduct were there and the flat cement platform. The little woods with large boulders and places flat enough to sit, the pool below the falls, and sandy edge where once all the sisters had wadded. We sat in the area where our Mom had sat writing letters and the family had eaten delicious picnics. It was like stepping back into time.

We had brought a little snack with us that we had purchased at a store in Hancock. We now sat in the rain and ate it reminiscing those long ago days with family. We had tears in our eyes as we spoke of those times.

It was when we were leaving this place of our childhood memory that we noticed the trash. Litter of various sorts: potato chip bags, soda cans, dirty, wrinkled notebook papers, a torn brown paper bag, a pair of purple swim trunks, several broken pens, a pile of used cigarette butts, etc. were strewn here and there.

Barbara didn't want to go without picking this litter up. So we did. We took a plastic bag that we had and cleaned up the area. It saddened us to see this area spoiled by human thoughtlessness.

Putting this last piece out of our minds we headed on to the camp in North Ferrisburgh having enjoyed a marvelous trip.

Instead of the usual four and one half-hours, to drive from my home in Connecticut to the camp in Vermont, it had taken us the whole day. All those hours were well worth the pleasure we had shared.

Figure 7 Dad Berger's favorite fishing spot – Bartlett Falls, New Haven River, Bristol, Vermont.

New Church

The Sunday after Barbara and my return to Vermont our friend Lorna called. She invited us to go to church with her at the United Methodist Church in 'the hollow'. She said, "I have just started going there and I love it. They have a new woman minister. You will really like her. Come with me this Sunday." So we did.

The service was outside on a beautiful sunny Sunday morning. We sat in chairs at the top of the hill behind the church facing a wonderful view of the New York Adirondack Mountains and Lake Champlain. The service was very impressive and the new minister, Mari Clark, an absolute delight.

For the children's sermon there was a live baby calf from John and Sue Devos' farm that Pastor Clark used as a prop and, of course, everyone thought this was great. The children named the calf, Mari. Mari's husband, Andy, also helped with the service.

What was truly impressive and important for my sister and me was that the people there welcomed us with open arms. Nearly everyone there made the effort to say "Hello" and greet us.

I have been attending United Methodist in these years since that day and my sisters do too when they come to visit.

* * *

Climb to the Summit of Camel's Hump—A Glorious Experience

In 1998 approximately forty years or more had passed since my Dad and Mom, my sisters and I, had climbed Camel's Hump. Longtime native residents also know this mountain as 'the couching lion.' Its elevation is 2084 feet.

On September 14th, 1998 after our return from Connecticut, Barbara and I made the decision that we would climb it once again.

We got up at 7 a.m., packed sandwiches, water bottles and a thermos of hot tea. We drove to Huntington Station, Vermont, about forty minutes away. We drove to the Burrows Cottage and the Burrows Trail entrance to Camel's Hump State Park. We parked the car and walked to the beginning of this trail. There we signed in the book for hikers, the date, the time and our names. It was 9:50 a.m. when we began our ascent.

Barbara led, being the eldest, to set the pace. We concluded that it would take us about four to five hours to reach the summit. Each of us carried a small satchel on our back and a walking stick. We hiked carefully, stopping about every twenty minutes to catch our breath. The trail went steadily, but gradually upward and in some places was slippery.

We discovered about a third of the way up that we did not have our water. We were not to be deterred and instead drank from the running mountain stream coming down along the hiking trail. It was more than refreshing. It was delicious!

We sang hymns from our childhood and quoted favorite verses of scripture such as in Psalms, 'I will lift up mine eyes unto the hills, from whence cometh my help. My help cometh from the Lord who made heaven and earth...' (Psalm 121) 'Bless the Lord O my Soul and all that is within me bless his holy name.' (Psalm 103:1)

Two young women came up the trail behind us about two hours up the mountain. They had started a half-hour after us they said and were on a tight schedule. They had a time constraint because of children in school. We persuaded them to take our picture at one of the clear spaces where there was a view through the trees. They had a friendly black dog, named Tess with them.

The summit of Camel's Hump is 2.7 miles. The Long Trail (a part of the Appalachian Trail system) crosses over about 2.4 miles up. Barbara and I arrived at this spot about three and quarter hours after our start.

The two women we had met earlier had already started back down. They had come to this point and turned around, not attempting the summit, because of their time constraint. We were tired but we were not going to turn around and not make the top!

We began our ascent to the summit, the last three tenths of a mile. The tree line was near and a variety of wonderful views became available as we hiked upward. We were in awe. We were delighted that we were going to make the summit. This part of the climb was now pretty much straight up and climbing up over rocks. God was with us and we knew this. We felt his grace and strength as we persevered.

We met several hikers on this last part of the trail. One group was a class from Norwich University, Norwich, Vermont and we met several young couples and single people. When we told some of them that we had last climbed Camel's Hump over forty years ago and that our ages were sixty-three and fifty-five, various ones congratulated us, wished us well and smiled. We were not embarrassed. For us this was a task we didn't know whether we would make but were determined to do.

At 1:50 p.m. Barbara and I reached the peak, the summit of Camel's Hump. Glorious! We gave thanks to almighty God for his encouraging presence, his grace, and strength. We gave thanks for this beautiful place of creation. We sang praises that we had persevered.

We had not expected anyone to be there. Forty-five years ago no one had ever met us on our climbs in the mountains and there had been no official state park. But now there were several little groups of climbers scattered over the bare rocky terrain. They were sitting or standing eating, viewing with binoculars or photographing the breathtaking, panoramic scenes surrounding us.

And an unexpected presence was a Vermont ranger whose job was to tell us about the ecological condition of the groundcover and rock formation. We asked him to take our picture on the very top.

Barbara and I found a spot and spread our little blanket out. We sat and ate our repast of sandwiches made with Great Harvest Bread and Vermont cheddar cheese, fresh fruit, and sharing a can of cold Sprite. We were filled with joy and a blessed awe as we took in the grand view all around us. To the West we saw the Adirondacks and Lake Champlain and we could see Long Point and the area where the camp is located. To the North Mt Mansfield, the highest peak of the Green Mountains. The city of Burlington and the village of Stowe, Vermont were in full view. To the East the White Mountains of New Hampshire with Mt. Washington and the three peaks of that range could be seen in the background of the Waterbury reservoir. Looking to the South, Stark Mountain, Mt. Ellen, and Mt. Abraham and the Green Mountain National Park Forest gave a spectacular view.

We could hardly believe that it was true! We were standing on the summit of Camel's Hump! We had achieved our goal! We sat in miraculous wonder and cried tears of joy and happiness!

We used the binoculars to watch a beautiful black raven travel in and out of the mountain air /wind currents. It seemed to float through the air; it's purple, black and blue grandeur of color as we watched. I thought it would be fun to fly like that!

Barbara and I spent the next forty minutes at the summit. We knew that we could not stay longer because it would take us several hours to go down the trail. Sometimes traveling down a mountain on the trail can be more hazardous than going up. Though breathing would not be a problem we knew we would have to be very careful on the steep rocky trail.

The ranger told us that a storm was brewing in the distance as well. The trail would get slippery with rain. We could see dark clouds rolling in from the West.

At 2:40 p.m. with 'Alleluias' and songs of praise on our lips we began our descent down the mountain trail.

I led the way as we began what was a three-hour trek down. We met several up-hill climbers on the way and stopped several places to see a last minute view. About half way down a gentle rain began and as the ground became more slippery, we were more careful. We did not mind the raindrops and commented about God's spirit raining on us.

We reached the end of the trail before dark and signed out in the book. I took Barbara's picture standing by the Camel's Hump state park sign. We sat in the car and drank our tea from the thermos.

What exhilaration! What joy! We could hardly believe that we had climbed to the summit of Camel's Hump once again after so many years. As we drove home we stopped to look back at the grand view of our mountain, Camel's Hump. It was truly a peak experience!

When I am at my camp during the summer season I walk to the top of my path. I look East and I can see this awesome mountain. I remember my childhood climbs to its summit with my family and I remember the recent climb with my sister. I use this thought to give me courage knowing God's presence will move me as I go forward to new heights each day in my life.

* * *

Another Friendly Visit

Toward the end of this first whole season our Connecticut friends John and Miriam came back to visit for the Columbus Day weekend. Though the weekend turned out to be wet and rainy we made the best of it.

We went down to the Dead Creek Bird Refuge in Addison County. Here in this valley along the Dead Creek the geese gather before heading south for the winter. I found it fascinating that the different geese gather at certain times. Whit and I had seen hundreds perhaps thousands of Canadian geese at the refuge there the previous weekend before John, Miriam and I visited.

On this day there were thousands of snow geese. This wondrous sight fascinated John. And while we stood watching them all of a sudden they began to rise in masse. What an awesome sight! All at once like a great white snow cloud they rose above us and flew off. Miriam and I watched John as he was mesmerized by this phenomenon.

We took a ride up into the mountains up over Lincoln Gap by Bristol and over to Warren, Vermont. We drove north up Route #100 and up through Mad River Glen on Route #17 over Appalachian Gap. The fall foliage was in its height of color and was spectacular!

We ended the day eating a delicious meal at the Dog Team Tavern, in Middlebury!

* * *

Ticonderoga Restoration

The Shelburne Museum celebrated a special day after the completed restoration of the Ticonderoga steamboat on September 26th. The McClure family had given 1.7 million dollars for the restoration of this historic steamboat.

Our friends, Mike and Lorna, with their friend, Margaret Titus, met Whit and me at the platform by the Ticonderoga steamboat at the Shelburne Museum. There was a dedication of the boat and then all in attendance were given the opportunity to walk through the newly restored vessel.

Mike told us how he had been a part of the crew as a sweeper for three years back in the 1950s and showed us where he had bunked.

There was a parade of steam engine vehicles including steam engine sailboats and 1920, 1930 vintage cars. Whit and I looked around for the model train display and discovered it no longer existed. We also looked for the stockade where my Vermont pen pal, Lynn Webster, and I had had our picture taken, but it was not there either. We found a building with historic toys and the building with models of circus paraphernalia was fascinating.

* * *

Mt. Philo Walkers

When Whit and I bought the camp in 1997, my friend, Lorna, had told me about a group of women who walked up to the top of Mt Philo in Charlotte, Vermont each day. She had organized this group after having walked herself alone for several years. She wanted me to join them. I did not go with them that first year.

However, at the end of September 1998 Lorna and her other friend, Margaret, convinced me to come along. I began walking the mountain on September 29th. I had twenty days to be a part of this daily excursion to the top of Mt. Philo. The distance is one mile and two-tenths, round trip a total of two and a half miles. The first three days I had trouble breathing but I made it to the top and the women were very encouraging. The fourth day it rained. I assumed they did not go. Never assume. These women climb/walk the mountain no matter what the weather is: sunny, rainy, and snowy weather. I guess from what I have been told the only days they don't walk, is in very bad icy weather.

And the following December 1998 proved to be a time when the mountain did suffer a bad ice storm.

Though the purpose was of course, exercise and better health, the walk to the top of this little mountain was worth every step. The reward is a spectacular view of Lake Champlain and surrounding Adirondack Mountains across in New York to the West and behind the mountain to the East, Camel's Hump and the Green Mountains.

Besides becoming reacquainted with this most beautiful mountain I made new friends with Lorna's friends, Margaret, Sue, Carol, Marline, and Donna. And though I have walked with this group off and on these several years and taken pleasure in the grand view of Lake Champlain and the Adirondacks I don't go often. Instead I walk the De Meter trail in Charlotte and the flatlands of Long Point.

* * *

Fish Story

Our friends, Carol and Paul, came to visit for a weekend. Paul likes to fish so Whit took him down to the cliff in front of the *Oak Ledge* camp. While he and Paul were standing looking out of the water huge fish were jumping. It was an exciting experience for both of them to see not one, but several fish jumping right up into the air in front of them.

We took them to Kingsland Bay State Park for a picnic as well.

* * *

The Main Street Bistro

Bob and Ruth L'Hommedieu had told my sisters and me about this restaurant in Vergennes on Main Street.

The Main Street Bistro is owned and run by two men. One man does the cooking and the other one is the server. The menu is selective but the food is quite gourmet. The atmosphere is quaint and classical music is played. The owners allow local artists to display their wares for periods of time. It is fun to go and eat there and see what different displays are being shown and sold. Whit and I had gone alone on occasion to this unique restaurant but we have liked sharing this interesting place to our friends who come to visit.

* * *

Evenings Out

Except when my sisters and husband, Whit, were at camp *Lottie* with me, I didn't go out much at night during that first full season.

However in October after I had begun going to the Methodist Church in 'the hollow', I went to the Tuesday night Bible study held in the evening at the parsonage.

Our friends Bob and Mary Gordon also invited me for dinner a couple of times and/or to play the game Skippo. Usually when I returned from any of these outings it would be after dark so I carried a flashlight with me in the car.

* * *

Skunk and A Fox

One night I came home from the Gordon's after a game of Skippo with Mary and her mom, Adele. It was a full moon. Coming into our driveway by the farm were two skunks having a mating session. I was glad I had driven my car and not walked. I would not have wanted to get them upset with me.

The very next night I went out again to a Bible study at the parsonage. The Bible study was a challenging experience as always.

When I came home at 8:30 p.m. I drove into the driveway. I didn't see any skunk this time but halfway across the pasture and up the hill to our camp I saw a large red fox loping down the drive. He was beautiful and intriguing. He stopped, stood still looking at my car and I thought, at me for a few moments before he ran off.

* * *

Big Birds, Hawks perhaps.

On a rainy, cold day, but just the same, a wonderful God made day, I was preparing to go back to Connecticut in three days. I wanted to get in as much of the lake as I could.

After eating a sandwich while sitting in the cozy living room watching the lake and rain, I decided to walk down and stand by the lake. I dressed warm and used Whit's raincoat and an umbrella. I walked down and stood on Ron and Alice's deck high above the water. The rain had stopped. I stood looking at the gray clouds with the Adirondacks of New York in the distance - Thompson's Point - still filled with the color of fall. The lake was excitingly rough with large white caps. I couldn't help but rejoice in the wonder of God's creation.

A big bird flew over, then resting in the airflow, glided by. Soon, another of the same kind of bird joined him as if to play, flying, then floating by. One after another other playmates joined in the fun. I thought "Oh, to join them in their play." I asked, "Are you getting ready for a bird show?" They seemed to go from one level of air current to another back and forth across Pleasant Bay.

In all, ten large hawks of some sort were flying and gliding sometimes in the same directions, sometimes moving back and forth some going one way and others flying almost into them. They flew off into the far distance and then back to near where I stood on my neighbor's deck. They were about twenty feet above me and with my binoculars I could see the glossy feathers of their wings, and brillant colors of brown, black, and white of their bodies. I was in awe and spoke to them of their gift to me.

* * *

Invitation to Preach

I have a seminary background so it was to my great delight when Pastor Mari asked me to preach on October 18th, Laymen's Sunday. I used the following scripture for the text of the sermon.

> 14. "You are the light of the world. A city built on a hill cannot be hid. 15. Nor do men light a lamp and put it under a bushel, bout on a stand, and it gives light to all in the house. 16. Let your light so shine before men, that they may see your good works and give glory to your Father who is in heaven."
>
> Matthew 5:14-16 <u>*The Holy Bible containing the Old and New Testaments with the Aprocryphal/Deuterocanonical Books*</u>, New Revised Standard Version, Nashville: Thomas Nelson Publishers, 1990.

I was pleased to sing a duet with my new friend, Sue, one of my favorite hymns, '*I Want to Walk as a Child of the Light.*' The words and music are by Kathleen Thomerson, 1966. This was a wonderful way to end my stay at camp that first full season. It was in fact my last day at camp for Whit and I closed that afternoon and drove home to Connecticut.

PART V

A YEAR OF TRAVEL - 1999

This second full season was the year of traveling.

Our first trip to Long Point at Bay View Road came the weekend of May 1st. Whit, our daughter, Torrey, and I had come up for the weekend to give a book event at the little United Methodist Church in 'the hollow'.

My book, *Choices A Journey Of Faith—Torrey's Miracle,* had been published in the spring and had come out in bookstores that month.

We had intended to stay at our little camp *Lottie*. However, the water had not been turned on. The pump system for the camps located at the Danyow farm was out. A new underwater receiving pipe was needed and later we found out that the primer pin had to be replaced.

We were in Vermont for a purpose, therefore, we stayed in the Skyview Motel in Ferrisburgh.

* * *

Camp Ready

The weekend of May 28th, Memorial Day weekend, we were able to open camp. Whit stayed for the weekend and I stayed for the next ten days. I went back to Connecticut for the second week of June because Torrey and I had another book event at the Barnes and Noble Booksellers in North Haven, Connecticut. I returned to Vermont to stay until September when several book talks were scheduled.

At the end of June I did drive to Holyoke, Massachusetts for the day where Torrey and I had a book event at the Barnes and Noble Booksellers. She drove from Guilford.

She came up again in September for an event at the Deep Leap Bookstore in Bristol, Vermont and we did a book talk and signing at the Barnes and Noble, Burlington on September 17th. We were pleased with the response to the event in Burlington and we were excited because a group from Franklin, Vermont called the Health Seekers videotaped the talk. They also invited us to come to Franklin to speak to their group.

I drove to Connecticut for a week in September and we did an event in Orange, Connecticut at the Barnes and Noble Booksellers there. Then we met again in Holyoke, Massachusetts for a second book signing in the same Barnes and Noble at the end of the month.

* * *

Baltimore Orioles

The birds in our little wood brought pleasure as soon as we were settled in for the summer season. There were two pairs of Baltimore Orioles living nearby. Actually one pair lived in their hanging nest right above the camp in a butternut tree. The branch they chose to build their nest stuck out over our roof. It was fun to watch the nest each morning as the mother came out to fly off and search for food. She would return and disappear into the oval shaped hanging nest. There seemed to be a lot of excitement inside as the whole nest would violently shake back and forth. My thought was always, Mom is scolding her babies. The male was so handsome with his brilliant orange breast and shiny black head and wings.

* * *

Visitors to Camp

During the summer I had several guests. My friend, Helen, came again from Connecticut for five days at the end of June. This year we fit in a Vermont Symphony concert with my friend Diane that was held at the Middlebury College stadium. We packed a picnic and took our beach chairs, candles and blanket and enjoyed a delicious meal while listening to the concert.

While Helen was visiting, my sister Barbara arrived to stay with me for a month. We went across the lake on the Charlotte Ferry to The Old Dock House in Essex, New York for dinner.

* * *

The Grand-puppy Comes to Visit

In mid-June into July I had the pleasure of taking care of the 'grand puppy', Quigley owned by our daughter, Jessica, and her husband, Dan. Quigley had visited us at camp the previous year with them. Jessica and Dan were going on vacation to Hawaii for two weeks. I was going to be in Vermont and would not be coming back to Connecticut so Whit and I took him with us a week before they were to depart.

Quigley, Whit and I drove up to Vermont on June 10th.

Quigley spent three weeks in Vermont and I grew quite fond of him. The following are stories of Quigley's time with us and with me.

* * *

QUIGLEY stories Journey to Vermont

The trip to Vermont with Quigley was without incident. The Peugeot station wagon was packed with Whit's painting equipment with a small space for the doggie bed and Quigley. We got up at 4 a.m. on that Friday and began our journey north. At the halfway point in Brattleboro we stopped to get gas for the car and to get coffee and a bagel at the Dunkin Donuts. I walked Quigley and he, of course, had to smell everything...every bush, every piece of debris on the road, every puddle of water, every car tire, every tree and why not, this is his nature. We drove on and came to our little camp *Lottie* by ten a.m. Quigley and I took a walk around the camp perimeters and farm.

* * *

The Oatmeal Catastrophe

Quigley fell into our routine immediately. Each morning I would get up between 6 a.m. and 7 a.m. Quigley and I would go out for his morning walk and 'nature's call'. We would come back and I would make coffee 'and' for Whit and me, breakfast of oatmeal and toast. Whit would begin his work on the camp, this year to scrap and paint the outside of the camp and I would work out in the rock garden areas. Quigley or 'Mr.' as I grew to call him, would go back and forth between us...with Whit on the deck or me in the gardens or inside if that is where I was.

One morning after our early walk I made the oatmeal, toast and coffee. My intention was to serve Whit up in the loft area where our bed is. I had given Quigley his breakfast and he was lying on the sofa near the loft ladder. I put Whit's coffee, toast, and oatmeal on a tray. I went to climb the ladder to the loft. It was not easy with the tray and I placed it on the rung of the ladder, moving up each rung slowly. I took the coffee off the tray and set it up on the floor next to Whit's bed. The bed is a mattress on the floor of the loft. I went to move the tray up one more rung. Somehow I missed, and the tray slipped. I caught the tray but the bowl of oatmeal went flying down to the bottom of the ladder in front of Quigley who had quick as a flash jumped off the sofa to get out of harms way. The oatmeal was of course everywhere. The bowl flew over the carpet and the oatmeal fell in a wave onto the carpet, the sofa and exposed wood floor. I had been told not to give our little grand puppy any people food. OOPS! Quigley managed to find every bit of oatmeal, cleaning the whole area perfectly. I thought he was quite the 'cleaning' puppy.

* * *

The Lake Experience

The third day Whit and I took our little charge down to the beach. Whit sat on a beach chair holding the long leash while I went out into the water. Quigley though a little leery came out into the water up to the bottom of his tummy. I was able to manipulate him into the water by pretending to run away from him. He immediately chased after me and of course the water got deeper. His little paws quickly began to paddle toward me. He realized instantly that he was getting farther away from shore so he turned around to go back toward Whit still sitting on the beach.

I spent quite awhile in the water and Quigley ran back and forth playing in the sand rolling and digging. Whit let him off the leash watching carefully to see where he went. He seemed to be enjoying being with us and did not wander off. After sometime I hooked him back on the leash and manipulated him back in the water so we could get most of the sand off of him. He seemed to get over his fear of the water and paddled around a lot. We went on little excursions like this several times with him during his visit. After each trip to the beach we had to bring Quigley back up to the camp and around to the deck and wash him off with the hose and/or several bottles of water.

* * *

Dog Walks

Speaking of walking with Quigley, we soon formed a special routine each time we went out whether it be morning, mid-day or evening. I would put the long leash on him and follow him out and up the path. When we got to the top of the common stairway that goes down to the lower path. Quigley would look one direction down the stairs and then up the path to the parking area and fields beyond. Then when he had made up his mind about which direction he wanted to go he would bound either up the path or 'quick as a wink' down the stairs. It was amazing to me how agile he was on the various stairways through the leased land area, especially with his short little legs. It seemed that he would choose to go up the path in the morning and down the stairway during the mid-day walk most days.

In the late evening about 9 p.m. or so just after dark, I would take Quigley for a last walk. He would go only to the top of the hill by our parked cars, do his 'duty' and turn around and run back down the path to the camp doorway.

The morning walk was usually fairly short, about ten minutes. We would walk up the path and around through the pasture to the lower area by way of the beach area back through the cedar grove. Quigley would find a secluded place in the bushes along the road and do his 'business'.

I found that Quigley is a rather modest dog. He would have to go in and under the bushes to complete his 'business'. If I happen to be looking his way, he would look back at me in such a stare as if to say "Please, give me a little privacy."

I would have to watch where he went so that the leash did not get caught in the undergrowth. Sometimes he would get the long leash tangled around the bushes and I would have to crawl in and get him untangled.

Mid-day walk lasted twenty to thirty minutes and on occasion longer if it was a cool day. We would walk down each of the stairways to the other camps on the property with Quigley sniffing every bush and tree. His favorite stairway was the cement stair in front of the yellow camp owned by the McGovern's, called 'Oak ledge'. This stairway goes right down to the water. We would get down to the bottom and he would carefully go down the last three steps and peer into the water, sometimes sticking one paw in, as if to test the temperature. He would then take a drink. Quigley could have easily jumped off these steps into the water. I tried to encourage him a couple of times but he never took the leap.

After drinking and checking each nook and cranny out Quigley would bound up the stairs with me in tow. Sometimes he would go so fast around the yellow camp where there is just a narrow ledge that I thought for sure he would run right off and would be hanging by his leash. I had to go pretty fast to keep up. We would go across the grass lickety split and he would stop dead in his track, turn and look at me with those mischievous eyes and grin. Sometimes he would grab hold of the leash in his mouth and run circles around me in playfulness.

Down on the rocky cliff of the 'common ground' Quigley would walk right down to the edge of the water, turn and look at me with that knowing look, as if to say, "I won't fall in, Grandma." Then he would lie down and sometimes we could see big fish swimming along the cliff's edge. On these occasions he would lay there five minutes or so, watching.

The path along the 'common ground' of the property leads to another dock behind the camp owned by the Bigelow's. Quigley would take me down along those rocks by that dock and explore the various nooks and crannies. I could never coax him to go onto the dock there because it was a floating dock and he seemed to be afraid of the movement. We would go back up the narrow path past this camp to the lower road and on to the beach used by the campers. Sometimes we would meet Monk the yellow dog owned by our neighbors the Bill and Ellen Bissonette. Monk would run up to Quigley in a friendly way. Quigley would snarl and growl.

My observation was that because he, Quigley was on a leash and Monk was not, that he had to make sure that he had the upper hand. Other dogs that we met on our walks out on the point who were on leashes would sniff Quigley in the same friendly manner as Monk and Quigley would be fine.

Our walk would continue down by the beach and back up the stairs there and around through the field making full circle back to camp *Lottie*. Going across the field we would often stop so that Quigley could roll in the grass or play with the leash.

When my sister Barbara came to visit she and I would walk each morning about 7:30 a.m. We would go up the path through the field to Bay View Road and down Long Point Road to Greenbush Road and back, about a three-mile trek round trip. Or we would go down the stairs and through the cedar wood to Annex Road to Long Point Road going out to the point and back, also a three-mile round trip. Quigley got into the habit of going with us. I would bring water with us for him.

He liked to go to out to the point I believe because he could run along the water's edge and go in up to his belly, drink and feel cool. It was very hot that summer.

On the long walks when he got tired, Quigley would just sit down or lay down and not move. I would have to give him a little tug on the leash. His little stubborn streak would occur on occasion and I would have to do more than give a little tug. He would look at us with a grin that said, "I am not moving. I don't want to go on. I'm resting, etc."

When we walked the long walks and Quigley went with us I always took water for him. However, I got tired of having to carry a container for him so he learned to carry his own water bowl. He would carry it in his mouth.

Figure 8 Top - Quigley with 'Grandma.' Middle - Quigley with water bowl. Bottom - Dan, Margaret, Jessica and Quigley

One day I forgot to bring the water so we stopped at the Bowles Factory next to the railroad tracks. I went in the back door and asked for some water. We got into the habit of getting water there in their kitchen.

* * *

Quigley's Bed

The first week that Quigley stayed with me I slept inside the camp on the sofa. He slept on his little bed by the side of me. However, each night as I would make up my bed he would jump up and snuggle down into the covers. I would have to coax him off and his sad little eyes would look up at me as if to say, "Don't put me out." Soon he began sleeping with me and there was not much room. When the nights got warmer I moved out to the single wooden bed on the screened-in porch. Quigley slept in his bed next to me because the bed was too high for him to jump up on.

At the end of the month when my friend, Helen, arrived I let her have the wooden bed and I slept on the rollaway cot. It was down low so Quigley once again slept with me rather than next to me.

* * *

The Deck

I had a concern about letting Quigley go out on the deck without the leash. It was like a big playpen to him. I worried about him sticking his head under the railing. We put a gate that Jessica and Dan had brought on the open end. It was a long drop down off the deck and when he ran I could almost see him sliding off. However he seemed to sense the danger and I soon let go of my fear.

It was fun seeing him lean his head out over the edge so that he could watch chipmunks, birds, squirrels play in the leaves and bushes below. Sometimes when other dogs went by he would get excited and jump up and bark...then my fear for him would come quickly back because he seemed to lean out farther over the edge of the deck.

Ninety percent of the time when Quigley was on the deck he would have someone with him. On occasion when I would be hanging out laundry in the side yard he would be on the deck. If the gate happened to be open he would run down the steps to play and if not he would stick his nose through the gate to see me.

I had to make sure he was closed in on the deck when I watered the flowers with the hose because he would jump after it barking and biting the end.

* * *

Lonely Quigley

Once in awhile I had to leave Quigley alone. I was fortunate only to have to leave him twice for long periods and two of my friends came to take him out for walks and spend time with him. I always gave him a piece of rawhide or a bone to chew on.

The first time I left Quigley was the worst. He jumped up and down on his short hind legs by the screened back door barking in a crying like manner as I was locking it. I kept picturing his sad little face as I was driving away.

The next time I went away I told him ahead that I was going to leave him and he seemed to understand. I put the bone or toy in the living room and would go. He didn't follow me to the door and so I felt better about it. I was always glad that he seemed to be happy to see me when I returned.

* * *

A Smelly Skunk

One night Quigley and I were alone and ready to sleep on our sofa inside the camp. I had a book that I was reading and he had his toy squirrel that he was playing with. Around 10:00 p.m. I was about to turn the light out when Quigley jumped up from his little bed on the floor barking. He jumped on the sofa and ran up next to me. I couldn't get him to stop barking. I realized that there was another noise too. I tried to get Quigley to stop barking so I could hear. Something was under the camp, directly under us. Quigley wouldn't stop barking and was getting more agitated.

At first I got frightened. But then... Oh the smell. It had to have been a skunk making all that noise, because it must have sprayed at the barking by Quigley and our moving around above it. Thank heavens it was outside. The smell was pretty strong but we were able to get through the night. Fortunately it did not bother us again.

* * *

Budlite and Quigley

Juliet was our neighbor for the summer as she was renting the camp next to us while her new house was being built in Jericho, Vermont. Juliet and her two sons were fine neighbors. They had a cute little Jack Russel terrier, Budlite.

Budlite, also referred to as 'Buddie', came to visit us with Julie on our deck a couple of times. Juliet and the boys had to leave Buddie occasionally and at the beginning it was hard for him. He got lonely and would bark. Only once did it get tiresome when he barked for over an hour during the evening. It was not an easy relationship between Budlite and Quigley but they became friends during those few weeks Quigley visited.

* * *

Barbara Comes to Visit

While my sister, Barbara from California, was with me in July we had some great times. The summer was pretty hot so we were glad when cooler weather popped up on occasion.

* * *

Canoe Lesson

When Barbara arrived that summer for her stay she told me that she had never paddled a canoe before. We had always used a rowboat as kids and/or went out in a small motorboat with our Dad running the motor.

So I said to her if you want to go out on the water you will have to learn to paddle. Her response was "I taught first grade for thirty-seven years. I am a pretty good listener. Just tell me in first grade terms what to do." And I did. She caught on immediately and we had many grand days out on the lake.

Once we paddled out to a spot between Thompson's Point and Kingsland Bay, on a smooth glassy lake. We sat for nearly an hour just enjoying the surrounding view, reading and talking without a care in the world. We paddled over and around the Dean's Islands and up the creek by Thorpe's Point.

* * *

Whit arrived for the 4th of July long weekend. I had gotten us tickets for the Fireworks Express train that was to run from Middlebury to Burlington with stops at Vergennes, Charlotte, Shelburne and South Burlington. Two trains would make this run: one at 6:30 p.m. and one at 7:30 p.m.

Whit, Barbara and I drove to Shelburne where we were to park our car and board the train. We took the later 7:30 p.m. train. We carried a blanket to sit on and a picnic for our supper.

Once we arrived we were shocked at the crowd, thousands of people already gathered on the lawns and docks of the Burlington Waterfront. We managed to find a spot on the rocky breakwater off Maple Avenue.

What a thrilling event! We had a great spot to view the fireworks that seemed to go on and on and on! Vibrant colors, sizzling, noisy, and grand, we were delighted and full of excitement at this spectacular showing. Of course the crowd's wonderful reaction to every burst of color and fast moving rockets up into the sky helped to make the atmosphere more exciting.

As soon as this fantastic celebration event ended, we walked less than five minutes to the Maple Avenue train crossing and boarded the Fireworks Express and headed back. An absolutely awesome evening!

* * *

A Lovely Breezy Day

July 12th was one of those days, a marvelous, beautiful day following five days of temperatures in the 70's and evenings of breeze and rain. On this day it was in the 80's with dry climate and blue sky.

Barbara and I did our daily walk along Long Point Road to Greenbush and back, leaving Whit to continue his painting of the outside walls of the camp.

She and I came back and spent some time writing letters and postcards.

We then went for a pleasurable canoe ride across Pleasant Bay and around the bay at Long Point. We chatted with Urban Saltus as we paddled by his sailboat on our way to their dock to talk to his wife, Elaine.

We returned to camp, made lunch of fruit salad and tuna sandwiches for the three of us. We sat and ate lunch on the deck while basking in the sun and taking in the lake view.

Leaving Whit to his painting project, Barbara and I drove to Burlington to do some errands.

I was trying to arrange for a book event at the Barnes and Noble Booksellers on Dorset Street. I was able to speak with the CPR, Community Relations Person, Nancy Namies, and we set a date for September 16th at 7 p.m.

Barbara and I returned to camp by 5 p.m. While we were sitting on the deck with Whit, Lorna stopped by with her little dog, Julie. And Juliet stopped in with Budlite. The two dogs got along quite well once they got through their dog sniffing routine.

This day had been busy, fun-filled, and blessed.

* * *

A 'Dog Rainbow'

Jessica called, a very nice surprise and we chatted for a few minutes.

Whit cooked hotdogs and veggie burgers on the grill that we supplemented with potato salad.

After dinner the three of us went out in the canoe just as the sun was going down. We were joyously surprised. As we paddled across Pleasant Bay to go across to Long Point we thought we saw a partial rainbow. But then Barbara noticed another rainbow. Each of these rainbows was on either side of the sun and we soon realized there were not two rainbows. Instead there was one rainbow going over the sun. This rainbow was in a horseshoe shape over the sun...incredible, beautiful and awesome. I have since found out that its name is a 'Dog Rainbow.' It slowly faded as we enjoyed the pleasantness of the lake for over an hour. An extraordinary sight and a grand day!

* * *

HOT Temperatures

After Whit returned home it got incredibly hot, hotter than I remember for Vermont. One day the temperature rose to 101 degrees. Barbara was very uncomfortable. She always wears long pants, where as I wear shorts. She would lie down on the floor lying still to keep cool.

* * *

A Heat Break

In mid-July God provided a break from the high heat. The sky was blustery with dark gray clouds and occasional sprinkles.

We had planned to go to Kingsland Bay State Park but decided with the possibility of rain we should stay at camp. We puttered around doing little things. We did a load of wash because we figured the wind would dry it. And it did. Barbara likes to do laundry so I let her. She had a special way that she organized the line, hung shirts on hangers, and the way she took down the clothes, folding them a certain way.

Half way through the morning we decided to drive to Bristol, Vermont and speak with the owner of Deerleap Books bookstore. I had made a connection with her the previous year. Now that my book, *Choices A Journey of Faith—Torrey's Miracle,* was actually out I wanted to reconnect and set up a date for a book event.

We had lunch at *The Bagel and Bakery* and on the way home stopped for groceries.

In the afternoon, since it was cooler I got the weed eater out and spent a while in the side yard sprucing the area. I watered the rock gardens and flower planters. Barbara spent time working in the side yard weeding and planting iris bulbs.

In the evening, just before dusk, we went down to the beach to get a bucket of pebbles to add to those on our path by the camp. We collected them and set the buckets aside so we could take a short canoe ride.

* * *

Evening Canoe Ride and a Neighbor's Swim

Kit Anderson who was renting one of the camps owned by Jack Danyow came along on an early evening canoe ride. She was ready for a swim so she went with us in the canoe around the Dean's Islands. On the way back she got out of the canoe along the edge of the shore and cliffs near the end of the northeast point. Barbara and I paddled along slowly while she swam. We picked her up again at Knowlton's dock for the last short leg of the ride across to the beach.

Before bed that night Barbara and I played Canasta. Barbara kept a running list of our games and who won/lost. She won that night, but throughout her stay we ran close.

* * *

Our Cedar Tree Friend

The next morning we woke to a beautifully cool day in the high 60's. The sun was shining on the lake slightly turbulent from a wonderful breeze. Following a breakfast of oatmeal, cranberry juice and coffee we put up more laundry, read while sitting on the deck and wrote letters. We took our daily walk.

We had originally planned to go to Kingsland Bay but instead decided we would take a picnic lunch, writing materials and books with us on our walk. We walked out toward the end of Long Point by the L'Hommedieu's and settled ourselves in a spot near our old friend, the cedar tree with the gnarled arm.

We sat and read, wrote in our journals and enjoyed the grand lake view. Of course the afternoon was too short because of the wondrous peacefulness that we always receive there.

Figure 9 Barbara Shock in canoe, Pleasant Bay; and in the arm of the cedar tree on Long Point.

* * *

A Meandering Trip to Chester

My friend, Helen, had bought me a stone birdbath, called 'angel kiss' from a stone works in Chester, Vermont. But I had to go pick it up. So one July day while Barbara was there we took a day to go pick it up and in doing so had a grand drive through the Green Mountains. We meandered all through the mountains to Chester. We drove up over Route #17 and Appalachian Gap down through the Mad River ski area and south down Route 100. We made a side-trip through the little village of Warren and on through the Granville Reservation State Park to Moss Glen Falls where we stopped for a lunch break having brought a picnic with us. We continued on through Hancock, Rochester, Stockbridge, Killington, and Plymouth to Ludlow. There we connected with Route #103 and drove east to Chester where we picked up the little birdbath.

On the way back to camp we went by way of Route #103 west through Ludlow, over to Cuttingsville and Route #7 to Rutland. Instead of going directly home we detoured over to Castleton by way of Route #4.

I wanted to show Barbara where my daughter, her niece Jessica, had attended her first two years of college. I gave her some of the history of the school as the first medical teaching facility and seminary, founded in late 1700s. I think it was 1791.

We drove north on Route # 30 along Lake Bomoseem to Sudberry, across 125 to Crown Point and the Champlain Bridge. We ate dinner at a family oriented local restaurant, The Bridge. This restaurant set up like a diner has come to be one of Whit and my favorites. We then went to Tooties, a carry out eating place for ice cream.

Barbara and I had been driving since mid-morning and when we arrived home after nine p.m. we were both exhausted from a very full and adventurous day!

* * *

Gentle Rain

The next morning we awoke to a much needed gentle rain. It soon grew to a steady downpour and cooled us off. It was wonderful! We spent the day reading.

* * *

Beethoven at Shelburne Farm

In July the Vermont State Symphony holds a series of concerts with guest instrumentalists known as the Mozart Festival. Barbara and I went to two of them.

The first one we went to was held on the grounds of Shelburne Farms. The orchestra was set up on the South porch of the former mansion owned by the Webb family. The spectators all sat on the lawn either on blankets and/or beach chairs. Most had brought picnics to enjoy either before or during the concert. We had brought our beach chairs and picnic supper. The program was the music of Beethoven.

While everyone was spread out on the lawn eating we decided to take a walk around the mansion grounds. There was lovely garden going down a hill toward the lake. As Barbara and I walked down some steps to this area we saw a young couple standing by the brick wall near the lake. We could here the conversation. The young man was proposing to his young woman friend and putting a ring on her finger. We almost felt like intruders during this special time, but it was also fun to hear and see this event.

After we moved back to our blanket and picnic and were just getting ready to eat our repast of salad and fruit, all of a sudden it began to rain. Everyone was jumping up and scattering and/or putting up umbrellas and/or covering themselves with blankets, summer jackets, etc. We didn't have an umbrella but threw our blanket over our heads. Barbara got red dye on her clothes and hands from the cover of the book that she had with her. Later, when we got back to camp she was able to get the stain out of her clothes and hands.

An announcement was made that the rain would last only a few minutes since it was a passing rain cloud. And it did only last about fifteen minutes. The concert took place as scheduled.

* * *

Kingsland Bay Concert

The next concert we went to in the Mozart series was held at Kingsland Bay State Park. This time we went with several other women: our longtime friend, Lorna; my neighbor near camp, Juliet; and Diane from Long Point. We took a large blanket, beach chairs and a fancy picnic. This picnic included food that each of us brought: deviled eggs, fruit salad, coleslaw, sesame noodles, blueberry muffins, zucchini chocolate brownies, various cheeses, salami slices and crackers, French bread, etc. We had wine and other beverages. These items were set up on a special picnic tablecloth with candles and flowers. It was great fun to sit near the water, listen to beautiful sounding music and visit with friends.

I had a swollen knee that was giving me some pain but with the aid of an ice pack from Juliet's cooler I was able to sit comfortably, listen to the concert and take part in the picnic. I liked watching the women interact with each other and took several pictures. One of them was a comical shot of Lorna with her mouth full of food.

* * *

The Murray's

One of the delights of the season was making a connection with our old friends, Charles and Shirley Murray, whom my family had known in the 1950s. Charles was the son of Mr. and Mrs. Alley Murray of Charlotte whom my family had known so many years ago. They came to our camp for a picnic on our deck with Whit and me in June. In July, Barbara and I had an opportunity to visit them in their home in South Burlington on a Sunday afternoon.

* * *

Peaceful Rain

After our visit with the Charles and Shirley, Barbara and I returned to camp and enjoyed the roaring deep thunder and lightening of a rainstorm that occurred in the late in the day.

We leisurely read books until it was time for dinner. It was still raining so we brought our meal out onto the screened in porch and ate by candlelight. The thunder and lightening had stopped but it was still raining. We liked to hear and watch the gentle rain and enjoy the quiet peacefulness of our little wood.

* * *

Juliet's Whaler

Just before Barbara went home, Juliet, our neighbor, took us boating…She had an old Whaler with a 70 horsepower motor that she took Barbara and me out for boating excursions.

One afternoon we went for a ride, found a spot on the lake where we could anchor and then swim.

Juliet is tall and slim. When we went swimming off her boat it was very easy for her to climb back in the boat using the motor to step on and then in to the boat. Barbara and I are not so lithe and we had trouble getting back in. It was kind of comical to watch us struggling. When we got home we both had bruises on our stomachs from getting in over the end of the boat.

* * *

Speedboat Ride

Our neighbors, Ron and Alice, have a fast speedboat with a 120 horsepower motor. They took Whit, Barbara and me out for a long two-hour ride up to Converse Bay, over to the New York side by Split Rock and back south to Basin Harbor. This ride was fantastic. Barbara was ecstatic.

On another early evening just before Barbara went home they invited us out for another long ride in water with white caps. We loved the bouncing of the boat over the choppy water!

* * *

Figure 10 Picnic at Camp - Charles and Shirley Murray, Whit Morse, Barbara Shock. On the Ticonderoga at Shelburne Museum, 1999 - Whit and Margaret Morse, Lorna and Mike Brown.

A letter to several friends in mid-July best describes the pleasurable events and days of that year.

Dear friends,

The summer is flying by. I have thought of you often since I last wrote and wondered how you all are fairing. I trust you are well and enduring the heat. It seems the whole country has suffered these heat spells.

My sister, Barbara arrived on Thursday, July 1st. Whit was here for the weekend of the fourth and we were able to do a couple of things away from camp.

We took the fireworks train express from Shelburne to Burlington Saturday evening to see the fireworks display over Lake Champlain. We got off the train and walked five minutes to a rocky shore area by the water to sit and watch the spectacular display. We brought a picnic in our cooler to enjoy as well. Of course the ride on the train was special as well.

My friend, Mari Clark, pastor of the little United Methodist church in 'the hollow' went to a family reunion so I took over the church service and I preached for her. The service was in the Center Church, Ferrisburgh. The two churches, the United Methodist of North Ferrisburgh and Center Church meet together in the summer.

It was my joy to have Whit and Barbara present and our good friend, Lorna.

I made another connection at church. Eleanor Palmer is one of the member's. Lorna often gives her a ride home from church and today when they were getting ready to leave I had a chance to speak with her. It was she and her husband who ran the Palmer's Store on Route #7 back when my folks and sister came to rent a camp so many years ago.

A forerunner of mini-marts, etc. my Dad used to stop there for gas for the car, gas and motor oil for the boat, and cigarettes. I am always amazed at meeting people here from those wonderful years.

Because it has been so very dry here I have to water my little rock gardens nearly every day. The irises that Barbara planted last summer have been beautiful. I have petunias and impatiens in my two flower boxes and geraniums in a hanging planter. The orange lilies and the yellow day lilies I planted by the parking area are now blooming and some Queen Anne's lace, Shasta daises and several unknowns. All are quite lovely.

We had marvelous rainstorms every evening for a week the second week of July. They cooled things off and we had 60 and 70-degree temperature instead of the 90 degree temperatures we had been having. The heat came back last Saturday and it hit the 100-degree mark on our deck.

Barbara and I have walked each morning three to four miles. We go to Greenbush Road inland, and back or down to the end of Long Point by the water and back. We have a routine of getting up between 6:30 a.m. and 7:00 a.m.; take our walk; returning for a breakfast of oatmeal, toast, coffee and orange juice; then writing letters and/or reading. We then have various choices of more reading, canoeing, working on the communal beach, swimming, occasionally going into Vergennes for groceries, water, and checking the mail. Walking early gets us back before the heat of the day.

The communal beach is for the seven camps located on the Danyow farm property. When Whit was here over the fourth, he and I started raking and collecting old lake weed and piling it up in the woods. Two of the other camp owners are now helping and we try to spend an hour or so each day on it. Jack came down several times to work with us for a couple of hours.

Of course it behooves all of us to help so that we have a clean beach to use. It will be a never-ending job, like dusting ones house, to keep all the lake weed disposed of. It will be a matter of spending an hour or so on a daily basis if everyone cooperates.

Barbara sat with a little paring knife digging weeds out of the sand while I hefted the pitchfork with lake weeds into piles for periods of time each day. We would finish and then go for a swim to cool off.

We drove to Montpelier to see our friends, Cindy and Mike Fessel for lunch on Tuesday a week ago. The following day we had lunch with Shirley and Charles Murray. Charles parents were my folks' longtime friends forty-three years ago. Allie, Charles' dad, ran the local car repair garage in Charlotte. He and our dad fished, mainly trout, together.

There is a fascinating connection between Guilford, Connecticut, the state of Vermont and the Murray family. 'Adirondack' Murray of Guilford history is in the direct line of Charles Murray ancestry. The Rev. William H.H. Murray of Murray Lane, Guilford began a Wilderness Camp in the Adirondacks, New York and so was nick named 'Adirondack.' He then came to Vermont. It has been fun sharing genealogy and local history of the Murray line in Guilford, Connecticut and Vermont with them.

Barbara and I packed a picnic lunch one day and drove to Kingsland Bay State Park (formerly the French school for girls) where we picnicked and swam in beautiful, clear, deep water. There are also hiking trails and boat rentals.

July 21st

I didn't finish this letter and two weeks have gone by. I'll try to finish now.

Whit arrived to spend the next week at camp. The three of us went down to the beach to rake and pick up lake weed again. Juliet, our new neighbor, Jack, and his granddaughter, Lydia, came to help too. Lydia cajoled me into helping her plan a beach party to celebrate all of our work. We are going to have a bonfire and cook marshmallows and hot dogs.

Whit has spent everyday until three and/or four p.m. painting. Three sides of the camp are complete, plus the camp walls inside the screened-in porch, doors and smaller areas. He has accomplished a lot. On days when it was really hot he walked around caulking holes in the walls.

There are so many birds in our little wood as always. A Baltimore oriole couple built a nest in the butternut tree just in back of our camp and we have enjoyed watching them and their brood. The nest hangs down from a branch and the birds go in through a hole in the top. Every time the female goes into the nest, it shakes. We decided that when she goes in, she is probably scolding her babies. One day we realized that the nest was empty and we did not know they had gone. We saw the male later going to a new nest. Orioles apparently do not have their second brood in the same nest and in fact usually go at least hundred feet away from the first one.

We have seen robins, blue jays, cardinals, red-winged black birds, grouse, various wood thrush, mocking birds, two redheaded pileated woodpeckers, other wood peckers, gold finch, morning doves, hawks, an osprey couple and their two babes, and humming birds, etc. I went to a bird seminar with my friend, Pastor Mari Clark, and I came home with a Roger Tory Peterson Bird Book and CD of bird songs. I hope that I can learn some of the calls and will be able to recognize the variety of birds we have in our wood.

Today July 21st, Barbara, our friend Lorna, and Mari Clark took the ferry from Charlotte to Essex, New York. We went to the Sunset Tea Garden for a delightful repast of English scones with clotted cream, strawberry cake and iced tea. Delicious!

We had a wonderful hymn sing down on the beach Thursday night. We invited the church people from both the North church and Center church to come. We had about twenty-three people. They brought their beach chairs and we made a bonfire. After we sang and watched a colorful sunset of variegated pinks, reds, purples and blues. We roasted marshmallows and made 'smoors' with graham crackers and Hershey's chocolate bars. Great fellowship and fun!

I leave for the Bahamas on August 6th leaving from Burlington to spend two weeks with Torrey for her tune-up. The IAT Centre is buying some books and I am going to do a book event for the staff and patients.

When I return Whit will be here for ten days. We will be going to a surprise 65th birthday party for Lorna on August 24th. Mike has arranged for a boat ride out on the lake leaving from Basin Harbor for about fifty or more friends. Everyone will bring a dish to share and we will have a picnic on the boat. It sounds like it will be great fun. Then I will be alone for two weeks before going home for a week for two books events at Barnes and Noble stores. We will come back for a week and closing.

I hope this epistle finds you both well and enjoying the summer! Keep cool!

Peace, Joy and Wellness,

Margaret

* * *

PART VI

THE YEAR OF THE BOSTON WHALER - 2000

A Letter to Friends from Camp Lottie

May 11th

Dear Friends,

This week has been rainy but has been a delight! Just being here in Vermont once again is great joy for me.

Whit and I arrived at our little 2-room hideaway nearly a week ago. We arrived at nearly 1 a.m. following a late start from Hartford, Connecticut. We had attended the first day of my Hartford Seminary Alumna Weekend before heading north to Vermont.

We went to the Friday evening dinner and to hear the main speaker for that evening, Matthew Fox. He gave a wonderful, thought-provoking address.

My book, *Choices A Journey of Faith—Torrey's Miracle,* was on display along with other alumni publications. No one from my class was there, but we met some fine people at the dinner.

Whit returned home to Connecticut after a few days having to go back to Page's hardware store.

I have worked an hour or so each day weeding the rock garden and iris bed on the south side of the camp and I have planted three planter boxes with impatiens and geraniums. The flowers in the rock garden are beginning to pop out.

I had forgotten what a grand season it is here since I missed it last year due to our plumbing hookup problems. All of the flowers are coming forth. Little buds of yellow, pinks, purple and blue are peeking through in the rock garden. The honeysuckle is coming out in pink and white and the iris that Barbara put in last summer will have dark purple blooms with white petals pretty soon.

This morning I sat several hours watching birds. A pair of mergansers with babies is in our little Pleasant Bay. The orioles are back, though I haven't seen the nest. You remember last year they had their nest in the tree just back of our camp. Blue jays, cardinals, robins, gold finches, a pileated redheaded woodpecker, red winged black birds, and purple finch are about. Also the gold and red hummingbirds are having a grand time hovering over the red impatiens.

What joy to be back as a participant at the little United Methodist Church in 'the hollow'! Lorna is singing in the newly formed choir and I will probably follow suit. I sang with them in April when Whit and I came to Vermont for the weekend.

Next Sunday everyone is to bring fresh baked cookies to be taken and given to inmates at a state prison. We are also to bring $5.00 for blanket Sunday. The monies will buy blankets for people in Turkey. This is a part of the outreach missions of the church.

This week my new friend, Michelle, from Guilford, a California transplant, and genealogy buff will be coming with her mom to stay for several days. Her Mom is flying in from Sacramento, California. They will use the camp as a place to rest at night while they hunt ancestors during the day. Michelle and her mom, Irene, will be searching for Fay and Fisk and Parmelee sir names. I may go with them and do my own research of Torrey and Marsh, sir names in Whit's and my family.

May 31st

As usual I didn't finish or send a letter started. I am going to add these last few days and send it off.

Whit has been back and forth from Connecticut and Vermont on weekends as usual. He will be coming for whole week periods this summer and this is much more pleasing for us.

Michelle, her Mom, Irene and I so enjoyed our trekking around Vermont looking up those long ago relatives. Near Richmond, Vermont we found a crossroads called Fay Corners and the hill where there was a Fay homestead. We thought there ought to be a cemetery nearby and as we drove down the road toward Richmond we passed a road going up a hill. The name of the road was Cemetery Road.

"Let's drive up that road," I said. We had gone about a quarter mile and didn't see any thing. However, an old man was walking down the road with his dog. We asked him if he knew of any cemetery in the area. "Yes," he said, "There is one." This man had never been in it or seen it but he knew where it was. "Down that hill and in those trees." We stopped the car right where we were and all of us got out and took a hike down the hill through the trees. We got out feet wet in a marshland area, but we did find a cemetery. We found a Fay cemetery with several generations of Michelle and Irene's direct line of Fays. Needless to say we were ecstatic! If we found nothing else that day we had already gotten a bonanza.

We went on to Richmond and spent several hours looking for more Fays and Fisks in the library and the town clerk's office. I helped them do some of their research but I also ran into some Torrey and Marsh records. The Marsh records were the same Marsh line as Whit's family of Marsh. We discovered later that this Marsh was connected to a Parmelee in Whit's Mom's family. This was the same Parmelee that Michelle and her Mom were searching for.

Since I have been traveling around the state with Michelle and Irene I have the genealogy bug again. It has been over fifteen years since I did the Torrey line for my family and Whit's Morse/Moss line with him. I would like to research more thoroughly the Torrey connections in Vermont and I want to see how the Guilford, Connecticut generations of people fit into this state's history. I know they do because the first governor Thomas Chittenden and his wife Elizabeth Meigs were both from East Guilford (now Madison), Connecticut.

I'll be in touch. Peace to you all,

Margaret

* * *

Rainy, but Cozy

Through the months of May and June there seemed to be a lot of rainy days and many weekends, especially when Whit was here. He had several outside projects to do and was getting discouraged.

It was often cold in the night but we did a lot of snuggling in the loft and that was nice. We would often use the two little oil heaters for a couple of hours in the evening to take the chill off. We would then get into our bed and stay there reading a book before going to sleep. In the middle of the night when I had to get up to use the facilities it was a little cool!

When my walking friends, Elaine and Mary, and I went out in the mornings we had to dress in long pants and sweat shirts to keep warm and carry umbrellas just in case it rained.

* * *

Spring Flowers

In mid June I was delighted when we finally had some bright, sunny days! The temperatures went up to the 70's during the day.

And my iris began to bloom! I counted nineteen blossoms the first day and more to come. Gorgeous! They were mostly all dark lavender with white petals trimmed with the purple on the edges. The rock ledge was in full bloom: Periwinkles in dark blue, Pinks, Shasta daisies, Solomon seal, wild Columbine and other little yellow and white flowers I don't know the names of.

When I look at this little garden I think of my Dad and the rock garden he would create over on the ledge by *Fleets Inn.*

* * *

New Friend and Neighbor

Our little camp is situated on Danyow Drive just off Bay View Road. This road ends just past the Danyow farm. There begins a long driveway that goes into a large piece of property owned by lovely lady, Doris Knowlton. She and her husband, Richard came to Vermont over forty-five years ago, settled there and raised their children.

I met Doris in the summer, 1999 and discovered that we had many similar interests including our great liking for the little United Methodist Church in 'the hollow' and of the people there. Her gardens provide many of the flowers for the services each week.

Through the winter Doris and I corresponded by letter through the United States postal service.

After I returned to camp this year I went to see Doris. However, she was no longer staying in her home but had gone to Pillsbury Manor an assisted living complex in South Burlington. I was disappointed not to see her. However I had a chance to chat with Doris by phone in her new living situation. We made plans for me to come see her on the day that she would be playing in the rhythm band. What fun it was to see Doris and the other folk playing that day and Doris and I had a delightful visit.

* * *

Mt Philo Breakfast

The Mt. Philo walkers sometimes get together for special occasions or birthdays. Even though Sue DeVos's birthday was in April, the group got together in June one morning for breakfast.

The walkers gathered at the bottom of the mountain and began their trek up what normally takes about a half-hour to the top. The rest of the group, primarily the men, drove to the top and cooked the breakfast using the outlets in the shelter.

The walkers got their walk in and we all enjoyed a delicious meal and some fine fellowship.

* * *

I wrote this poem on a lovely warm day in June while I was visiting this particularly nice Vermont spot.

KINGSLAND BAY—a place of beauty

Sitting on the grassy lawn I watch as a canoe
    slides into the glistening water,
    the young couple unaware of my presence.
The dark, blue-green water lapping against the rocky shore
    waits to take them to new adventures.

I thought, what delight for them to be out there
    on that sparkling lake
    without a care in the world, but each other.
The sun shone down caressing and warming
    their skin, now brown from many such days.

The gentle wind making a slight breeze
    causes the many colored flags of nearby boats anchored,
    to fly.
The American flag just there on the shore
    gives a sudden burst hailing its stars and stripes.

In the little cove nearby, two Canadian geese
    herd their babies under a rocky ledge shelter,
    away from a motorboat speeding by.
Overhead more ducks fly, squawking.

A rustling sound occurs.
    Behind me a little brown garter snake
    slithers into dry brown leaves,
    just his tail end showing.

Across the cove a sailing crew readies their boat
    moving it away from its mooring.
It motors out of the little bay to the broad lake
    where the wind has begun to blow.

Walking along the cliff edge I follow the wooded trail
around the point to view the broad lake.
There in the undergrowth a red fox spies me
and looks directly, with no fear, into my eyes.

This place of natural beauty has its history.
This land, once privately owned, the stone structure
a family home and an Inn for travelers.
A ferry to New York was provided.
A place of housing for militia during the war of 1812;
then a monastic retreat;
And later a school for girls studying French;

Kingsland Bay, on the shores of Lake Champlain
is now a Vermont State park.

Margaret Torrey Berger Morse, June 2000

* * *

Family Connections through Genealogical Research

I did what I said in my letter to friends. I went to Georgia and Georgia Plain up on the mainland near South Hero to look for Torreys. I found a Torrey Cemetery and the house of Capt. Brown Torrey at Milton's Landing on the lake.

I invited my Long Point friends, Elaine and Diane, to go with me to Royalton, Vermont to find where Dr. Joseph Torrey, D.D. had lived with his wife for several years. Diane was kind enough to do the driving. They were both very patient with me, as I wanted to stop at every cemetery along our route.

I had hoped to find his grave. I didn't find the grave but did find information that proved he lived in that community for a period of time. He had been the minister of a church there.

Dr. Torrey was the ninth president of the University of Vermont. I had looked for his grave at the Green Mountain Cemetery in Burlington first because several of the UVM presidents are buried there near where Ethan Allen and family are buried. Dr. Torrey's nephew, Augustus Torrey, is buried in that cemetery. Augustus taught at UVM after Dr. Torrey was president and he married his first cousin, a daughter of Dr. Torrey. Augustus later went west to Idaho and it may be that it was he who founded the town of Torrey, Idaho.

One of the older buildings on the UVM campus is named the Torrey Building after Dr. Joseph Torrey, D.D.

I also did some research in the University of Vermont Library and Archives on Dr. James Marsh, D.D. This man was the fifth president of UVM and his ancestors are connected to Whit's family by marriage.

Dr. Marsh and Dr. Torrey were good friends. I found this connection between our families fascinating. I found written material that speaks of these two men's friendship while they were students together at Dartmouth College, again at Andover Newton Seminary and then while they were both professors at UVM.

Dr. Joseph Torrey, D.D. compiled all of Dr. Marsh's writings into a book after his death. Dr. Marsh died of consumption at age 48. There was a copy of this book in the UVM library. Dr. Marsh being a Transcendentalist helped Coleridge get established in Vermont.

My next task was to find if there was a connection between Dr. Joseph Torrey, D.D. and the Torrey family I found in Georgia Plain.

By the end of the summer I found that the Georgia Plain Torrey family were probably descendents of a Torrey line that came from Scotland via Nova Scotia.

Dr. Joseph Torrey came from Beverly, Massachusetts and was probably descended from Capt. William Torrey who settled in Weymouth, Massachusetts. Capt. William Torrey's brother, Lt. James Torrey who established his family in Scituate, Massachusetts, is my direct line. These brothers and two others, Joseph and Philip Torrey, came from Somerset, England in the early 1600's.

* * *

Guilford, Connecticut Connections

I did find some exciting information through the many death records in the Georgia Town Hall, the one in St. Albans and in Williston that I found awesome. The people whose death records I read, many of them were born in Guilford, Connecticut during the 1700's and 1800's. I know that I will have to do much more research in this area … connecting Guilford, Connecticut to Vermont. And I will. Perhaps that will be another book.

It is my guess that you may have to be fascinated by wanting to know your roots and enjoy this kind of genealogical research to read these meanderings.

* * *

Friends, The Old Dock House, and Air Balloon Entertainment

One bright weekend in June my niece Jenny, my sister Jeanne's daughter, came to visit me from Boston. We were enjoying relaxing together on the deck when two friends called.

Janet and Eliasz Poss are my neighbors from home in Guilford, Connecticut. They were on their way to visit other friends in Richmond, Vermont and called to see if they could stop by to see me for a couple of hours. I had told them to come by anytime. "Come ahead," I said.

After Janet and Eliasz arrived the four of us sat out on the deck and chatted, had cold drinks and enjoyed the view of the lake. They had never seen Lake Champlain.

Jenny found this couple fascinating, as do I. Janet and Eliasz's conversations are always profound. I was very pleased that they took the time to stop by.

Jenny and I had planned to take the Charlotte ferry across the lake to The Old Dock House restaurant. We asked them to join us.

They followed us in their car to the ferry parking lot. We parked and went on the ferry as walk-ons. The ride across the lake was pleasant though the water was fairly choppy and it was a warm and sunny day. I was glad that my friends could experience the grandeur of the lake and see the splendid view of both the Green Mountains and the Adirondacks.

Once we were at the restaurant we settled in to ordering our dinners, chatting and eating. At some point one of us looked up and there across the lake were balloons, large air balloons. We counted eight. One of them was the Energizer bunny and another I recognized as the one that has the Vermont scene of the mountains and a rainbow.

I remembered then. This was the weekend of the Balloon Festival at Essex Junction, Vermont.

I could not have planned better entertainment. And I had my binoculars with me so each of us had opportunity to look closer. There was a couple with their two little girls at the restaurant and we shared the binoculars with them.

In all we had an extraordinary lovely day!

* * *

Surprise Visit to Illinois

At the end of June Whit and I flew to Illinois to attend my sister, Jeanne, and her husband, Paul's, 40th Wedding Anniversary. It was a surprise party setup by their three children Lori, Wesley and Jenny. A great party and a blessed family reunion!

* * *

Return to Vermont

Arriving back in Vermont in July Whit and I had missed getting tickets for the July 4th train to see the Fireworks in Burlington. However, Whit and I had fun cooking steaks out on the grill and watched another spectacular Vermont sunset.

I enjoyed going out in the canoe with Whit each time he was here through the month. There is nothing better for me than being out on the lake. We looked for beaver while paddling up one of the inlets when we saw a beaver house. We saw blue heron as well as red-winged black birds nearly every time we went out in the canoe.

* * *

A Trip to Maine

In mid-July I drove Elaine from Long Point to Portsmouth, New Hampshire to visit her daughter Cassie and husband, the Rev. Christopher Robinson. The three and a half hour drive across Vermont and New Hampshire gave us a chance to see the mountains, Green and White and to visit.

Once we arrived, Elaine and I drove down to the waterfront and walked in a park built along the ocean and by a local harbor where there were sailboats and large seagoing vessels. There were gardens in bloom and an outdoor concert was taking place on an outdoor stage. We saw a wedding party having their pictures taken and people arriving for the wedding that was about to take place in one of the formal gardens. We could look across to Kittery, Maine.

That evening for dinner Cassie served lobster that was delicious and melted in our mouths. Elaine was staying a week but I stayed just the one night and then began my journey back.

I left about ten the next morning and drove south down I 495 into Massachusetts. I met my niece, Jenny, for lunch in Lawrence, Massachusetts. We walked, ate lunch and visited for two hours before I headed up I93 into New Hampshire and west to Vermont for a most enjoyable ride home.

I have traveled to various parts of our nation and each area has its own special beauty: the majesty of the mountains in Rocky Mountain and Glacier National Parks; the starkness of the Sierra Nevada Mountains; the serenity found in the vast Plains of the mid-west; the awesomeness of the Grand Canyon and southwest; the tropical climate of the Everglades; and so much more. But for me… New England. It is the best!

* * *

Concert at Kingsland Bay

Lorna, Pat, Diane, and I had a delicious repast and another fun evening at the Kingsland Bay Mozart concert at the end of July.

I love watching people and at an outdoor concert like this. It was fun for all of us to see what food and drink people brought, how elaborate their picnics, etc. Some people brought little tables, cloth, candles, wineglasses, wine, champagne, hors d'oeuvres, in other words 'the whole works'. We saw one group of people who had candelabra set up on a table with a very fancy cloth, china and silver. It was very elegant to say the least.

I caught Lorna with her mouth open again and took another great comical shot.

Many concert attendees come in their various boats and we saw motorboats of many sizes and a variety of sailboats. There were even several people in kayaks.

* * *

Anniversary Surprise Disappointment

When I returned home that evening a message was waiting for me on the phone message machine. It was from the Millhouse Bed & Breakfast, a quaint B & B on Lewis Creek in Starksboro, Vermont.

I had made arrangements for Whit and I to go there for our 33rd wedding anniversary in August. It was to be a surprise. They called to say that they had been struck by lightening in one of the thunder and lightening storms on July 15th. They had to cancel our weekend because of the damage. I was so disappointed but they reassured me that they intended to restore the building and would be open for business in 2001.

* * *

Another Letter to Friends

August 11, 2000

Dear Friends,

We have warm weather and only tentative storm clouds over the mountains. It has been raining often as I have mentioned before. But you know me I LOVE VERMONT no matter what the weather!

I returned to Guilford, Connecticut a week ago, Sunday, July 30th. I had preached that morning at the little North Ferrisburgh United Methodist Church on the hill in the 'hollow'. Pastor Mari was away on a teaching mission in Rutland, Vermont.

After church I drove home so that I could be there for Jessica's 29th birthday celebration, dinner with the family. Whit's Mom, sister Jane, Torrey, Dan, Whit, Jessica and I went to a restaurant in Old Saybrook, the Oyster House.

Most of you know that Torrey bakes delicious and wonderfully decorated cakes as a side hobby. She had made one for Jessica and brought it to the restaurant. The manager was very kind and allowed us to serve it. Torrey also served our waitress and other servers some of the cake.

I had a week to catch-up with Connecticut friends and went out to breakfast one morning with Jessica.

I returned to Vermont on August 6th for two weeks.

Tomorrow is the first annual LOBSTERFEST for the United Methodist Church. Nearly the whole church family have been involved in its planning, advertisement, and now the actual event. Dot Mills and M. Jane Palmer have baked a variety of pies along with several other women. The menu consists of lobster, corn on the cob, potato salad, coleslaw, and rolls, pie and a beverage.

Hot dogs are also being offered for those family members who don't like lobster and/or prefer hot dogs. Whit is helping with the cooking of the hotdogs while I work as a server.

I think we have nearly a 150 reservations. And we have enough lobster for walk-ins. There will be games offered for kids who attend. This event will happen rain or shine and it looks like the forecast is calling for some rain.

I found working on the Lobsterfest committee amiable because money was not the main focus. The purpose was to create fellowship within the church family and to be an outreach to the community. If the event makes money it will be a bonus.

Our friends, Ellen and David from Middlebury, may come and stay at the camp again while I am home at the end of the month. Jessica, Dan and friends will also come on the 18th for a weekend in my absence.

I am going home to be with Whit when he has his hernia surgery and for a week of recovery. He will then come back with me for two more weeks of recovery time.

I am having a fantastic time taking friends for rides in the new Boston Whaler. I took Mari this afternoon. My sisters are going to love this boat. I can hardly wait for them to arrive. We are going to have a blast!

The sunset is beginning to fade.

Enjoy the rest of your summer.

Peace,

Margaret

* * *

The Blueberry Pie

One of the women at church, Char Irion, had made a cold blueberry pie, quite unique, for the Lobsterfest. When she got to the event someone had taken the pie and put it into a refrigerator in the back of the kitchen. When the Lobsterfest was over she came to get her pie pan. No one knew where it was. Then it dawned on someone that her pie was still in the back refrigerator. The pie was taken out and immediately eaten by the clean-up crew most of whom had not had dessert. The pie was more than delicious! The result was that the clean-up crew wanted Char to make this pie again for next year's Lobsterfest and save it for them.

* * *

Birthday Surprise - Doubled

Pastor Mari Clark was planning a birthday surprise for her husband, Andy's 50th to be held at Cactus Pete's Restaurant in South Burlington. After I shared with her that Whit's 62nd would be around the same time she graciously let the surprise be a double birthday. Close friends and family came, about twenty in all. A grand time!

* * *

Purchase of the Boston Whaler - 2000

When Whit was with me in mid-July we were sitting one evening having a glass of wine and enjoying a cool breeze, while watching a Vermont sunset.

He said to me something like "Don't you think it is about time you bought that boat you have always wanted?" My reply, "How? What will I use for money?" He said, "Do you remember the stock your Mom left you?" "Yes,' I said. "It was worth about $1,600." He said, "It has been ten years and it is worth more than that now." It just had never occurred to me.

So to make a long story short I went boat hunting. My Long Point friend, Diane Eisenhower, went with me. We looked at used boats and then we went to North Hero, Vermont to Northland Boats. I had gotten on the Internet and had checked out Boston Whalers. They sold them there.

Diane and I had a delightful day driving to North Hero and seeing the islands. We went to Northland Boats and looked at different Whalers. I did not purchase anything then, just took information. There was a new 13'3" Boston Whaler sitting outside the main building. We looked at it closely. I thought this is just the size for me. It had a 30 HP Mercury motor on it. The salesperson Ron Tier gave me his take on the boat.

We left the boat store and spent time driving around the area. We stopped at a hotel/motel restaurant very elegant dining room to eat lunch in North Hero. We ate outside on the patio looking at the lake. Because we were on the east side of the island we were looking at the Green Mountains and my favorite mountain, Camel's Hump. The treat of the day was scrumptious strawberry shortcake. I don't remember what else we ate.

Whit and I figured out what to do with the stock - there were lots of little ones. We sold enough stock that would cover what I would need to buy a 13'3" Boston Whaler with the Mercury motor and boat trailer. When I went back to Northland Boats with Whit they did not have any in storage. So one was ordered one for me.

The Boston Whaler, a 2001 model, 13' 3" Sport with a 40 HP Mercury motor was delivered three weeks later by the salesperson, Ron Tier, from Northland Boats and his wife, Joanne.

* * *

Jack Danyow from the farm and one of the other camp owners, Bill Bissonette, helped me put the mooring in the day after the boat was delivered. I wanted to make sure the mooring was put in our little bay where Jack recommended. Whit was in Connecticut and Bill had a big boat. So one evening he took Jack and me out and they did the job. Bill then gave us a lovely ride on the lake in his large boat, 'the Grey Goose.' Wonderful!

* * *

We didn't get the whaler in immediately, but within a week. Ron and Alice, our camp neighbors, came on a Friday with their Jeep and trailer hitch. They hooked up to the boat and trailer. We drove down to the bay at Long Point. Ron and I went in the boat taking it around the point to the mooring and Alice drove the Jeep back to camp.

I had taken my canoe and hooked it up to the mooring earlier in the day. I had paddled it out, tied it on to the mooring, jumped into the lake and swam back to shore.

Ron and I brought the boat up to the beach where Alice was waiting. They helped me put the letters for its name, the registration letters and numbers, and Vermont sticker on it. I named the boat *CHOICES* after all the choices I have had to make in my life, the choices Whit and I have made together, and those we make each day.

* * *

Needless to say, I was like a kid with a new toy. We had eight weeks to use *CHOICES* before the end of the season. I had to go home for two weeks at the end of August. But I had six grand weeks of boat excursions before we closed camp and secured the boat for the winter. WOW! Thank you Mother!!

* * *

First Boston Whaler Adventure

It was essential to learn all the parts, the mechanical workings, etc. as the owner of this new Boston Whaler. I typed the steps for preparation and running in bold letters and had the paper laminated so I could keep it in the boat.

The second day that I had *CHOICES* in the water and actually running it my friend, Lorna, came for a ride in the boat with me. My canoe is the boat that I was using to get from shore out to the whaler. We put all of the essential equipment in: floating device (a cushion); life preservers, registration, boat manual, etc. Lorna paddled with me in the canoe over to the mooring.

We had our first boating adventure! I got into the boat put the plug in and then sat and read through the procedure of what to do to start the boat and get underway. Lorna got in and we put our life preservers on. I went through the procedure doing each step and then we started out.

We were on our way around the point to Diane's camp to pick her up. We would all go for the initial first ride. Well, half way around the point as I began to pick up speed all of a sudden the plug popped right out.

"Oh..@#%$….!" was my reaction. Lorna grabbed hold of her life preserver tight and shouted "Are we going to sink!"

And the look on her face was that of fright and surprise! "No," I shouted back. "I can put this plug back in." But guess what? It would not go back in tight. So I put my foot on it to hold it down and proceeded on to Diane's. I thought she might know what to do.

Well we ended up driving over to the Point Bay Marina with my foot on the plug the whole way. I was able to buy another plug, but the young man there said, "You don't need another plug. Let me show you." The washer had come loose and just needed to be tightened and then we were on our way for a fantastic ride on Lake Champlain!

* * *

More Boating Excursions

The next several boat excursions took Diane and I out on the lake to find places where we could anchor and swam, explore beaches for driftwood, see birds such as the blue heron along the shore and take long rides out on to the 'broad lake' etc. Lorna couldn't come too often, but when she could, she did.

* * *

Sister Reunion - 2000

After my sisters were here for our Vermont reunion in September I wrote this poem.

The Year of 'the Whaler'

Here we are again
    The three sisters and I.
At camp on Lake Champlain
    Oh me, Oh my!

Our fourth reunion,
    This, the third on the lake,
Always a joyous occasion,
    Certainly never faked.

This week so very special,
    Each day filled with sibling fun.
Walking the road around Long Point,
    Also the new DeMeter Trail.

Chatting, singing,

Playing cards together.
Visiting with Vermont friends.
Enjoying fine dinners at The Old Dock House
Uno's, and The Main Street Bistro.

Driving through the Green Mountains,
This one-day adventure.
We enjoyed the exquisite view at Appalachian Gap.

On through Mad River country
And down Route #100
Stopping at Warren
That quaint little village.

On to Moss Glen in the Granville conservation area
A first visit to Texas Falls
Both so very splendid.

We ate our picnic fare
Watching the water's mist
Oh so superb.
Walked and climbed paths
More carefully than the past.

Across #125 toward East Middlebury,
A lovely drive
North again toward Bristol.
We visited one of our Dad's trout fishing spots.

But the GRAND times
The best, being out on the lake.
Each day a ride if possible
in the new 'Boston Whaler'
CHOICES gave the greatest delight!

October 2000

Figure 11 The Boston Whaler - 'Choices'. Margaret Morse and Ron Gabriel. Margaret Morse and husband, Whitney Morse, 2000.

Figure 12 Sisters enjoying 'The Boston Whaler': Barbara, Bobbie, Jeanne. Margaret swimming. Alice Gabriel, 2000.

Figure 13 The Old Brick Store, Charlotte, VT. Sisters on the porch. The Ethan Allen Spirit II Ferry.

Figure 14 Pleasant Bay with ducks; Sisters: Back to front Jeanne, Margaret and Bobbie.

Figure 15 Sisters: Bobbie, Barbara, Lorna Brown (Friend), Margaret and Jeanne at the Old Dock House Restaurant, Essex, NY, 2000. Alberta sitting on 'the rocks' Long Point.

* * *

Jeanne's Gift - 2000

While my sisters were visiting we had the privilege of singing for the United Methodist church one Sunday morning as a quartet. After sisters Barbara and Bobbie returned to their homes Jeanne stayed on a few extra days. She gave the congregation a gift of a solo. She put into a melody several of the old church hymns from our childhood days and sang it for them. I am always delighted to hear Jeanne sing but what stirred me most was seeing her faith that always shines forth.

* * *

Whit and I were introduced to Jane and Bruce Werner, a delightful couple living in the *Lakeview* camp on the corner of South Road. This camp owned by Bruce's family was built by earlier generations in 1897.

My husband and I were pleased in getting to know this couple now retired and living on Long Point summers and in the Bahamas during the winter months.

* * *

Nearing the End

When the time gets near the end of the season I am still awed that we have been so blessed to have this little place of retreat, 'Camp Lottie' on Lake Champlain. Whit and I seem to cherish all those last days the most, knowing we will soon go home for the winter months.

In that last week we enjoyed the company of our friends Charles and Shirley Murray when we attended the Annual Thanksgiving dinner put on by the Baptist church in Georgia. It is a dinner they have served and done well for over forty years.

* * *

We also went to Ron and Alice's new home for a wonderful grilled salmon dinner in Essex Junction, Vermont. Their home looks out over a pasture with its backdrop being the grandeur of Mt. Mansfield and the mountains of that region.

On our drive to their home we experienced a magnificent site. The foliage was in full color so we took the back roads up through Monkton, Hinesburg, to Huntington and north to Richmond, Jericho Center, Underhill Flats, then north on Route #15 to Cambridge. We then drove across #104 and south on #15 to Essex. Junction. The drive was exquisite. The colors were brilliant: various shades of red, yellow, gold, rust and brown.

It had snowed the previous day or two up in the mountains so that we also had the contrast of the white snow covered mountains…Camel's Hump and Mansfield, and those in-between.

This wondrous drive through the mountains of color and snow is one that I savored during the winter back home in Connecticut.

* * *

Camp Closing and CROP Walk

We closed camp on the third Sunday of October. After church Whit drove home and I stayed to walk with the people of United Methodist in the CROP Walk in Burlington. I had the privilege of organizing the walkers from the church and wanted to be there.

The Youth Group, through the fine leadership of Sarah Hollier, had helped me put together a presentation in the morning service. They did a very fine job!

* * *

December Visit - A Surprise Birthday in Vermont

Whit and I received an invitation from Andy Clark, Pastor Mari Clark's husband, to a surprise 50th Birthday Party for her. The party would be on the actual day, December 8th. We decided we would drive to Vermont.

The day was a Friday so we left in the mid-morning and drove north. We went to the camp first to check it out. Everything was in order. We couldn't stay there but it was fun to drive down and see how things look in December.

The party was a complete surprise for Mari! Everyone from the church was invited, other friends and family. We all gathered early in the 'upper room'. This is a new room, part of an addition built within the last five years.

I had my camera and what fun to take pictures of the very real surprised expression on Mari's face. Mari knew that the Boy Scouts were having a special gathering that evening. When one of the scouts came to the parsonage and said she was needed, she went.

The party was a success from the beginning to the end. It included a potluck dinner in a beautifully decorated hall by several women of the church. Over a hundred were in attendance. After the meal a sharing of memories of Mary was done. This became quite comical.

Whit and I spent the night and were blessed to have the opportunity to go back to church the next day and help decorate it for the Christmas season and to fellowship with our Vermont friends. We enjoyed an evening out including dinner with some of them.

We planned to go back to the motel and then go to church the next day. Our friends, Stan and Carol Smith, offered their home and so we canceled our reservation at the motel.

The Smiths live up on Mt. Philo Road in a lovely home that has a panoramic view of the Green Mountains including Camel's Hump in the front. I could be envious of this setting.

They also have in the back of their home the grand view of Lake Champlain. These views are incredible! Their hospitality was very gracious.

And on Sunday morning we visited the church again for the first Sunday of the Advent and Christmas Season.

We returned home taking with us another pleasure of Vermont!

* * *

Part VII

THE ADVENTURES CONTINUE - 2001

April Trip to Vermont

At the end of April Whit and I drove to Vermont and spent the weekend. We stayed at the Country Side Motel, Shelburne, Vermont.

In past years when we would drive to Vermont we would stay at JIMMOS Motel on the corner of Route #7 and Hollow Road, North Ferrisburgh. However, in recent years when we have gone to Vermont in the Autumn or early Spring this motel has not been open. And even now in the summer it is open but has been for sale for at least two years or more.

JIMMOS store was across the street but three years ago it was sold and torn down. Now there is a Mobil Short Stop in its place. I guess this is supposed to be a sign of progress and change.

* * *

I had been to the IAT Centre in Freeport, Grand Bahama Island, Bahamas in March to help a friend get started as a patient at this Cancer clinic. When I returned home I brought home serum to deliver to our friend Betty, who had moved to Williston, Vermont.

When we came in April it was so that Whit and I could deliver the serum to her. We had a good visit with her and a delicious lunch at Evergreen Eddy's Wilderness Grill. As always it was a special treat to go to Vermont before the summer season.

* * *

A Car Dilemma

While in Vermont we of course took the time to stop at camp and check things out. Jack Danyow was standing outside his house when we pulled into the driveway of the farm. While we stood talking to him he had a telephone call. His neighbor and friend to all of us, Doris Knowlton, was in a dilemma.

Doris had moved home from the assisted living situation of the previous year. She and her caregiver, Connie had taken a drive down to the lake so that Doris could see the water.

It had recently rained for a few days and the field they had driven through was still pretty wet. They had made it to the lake okay but on the way back they had gotten stuck in the mud.

Jack, Whit and I went over in our car to see what was needed. The three of us worked the car that Doris was sitting in back and forth so that we could push it out of the mud hole while Connie drove. Doris was having fun I think because she was laughing. The situation was pretty comical.

Our rocking the car didn't work. We did a scavenger hunt to see if we could find something to put under the tires. Whit had some metal grated pieces in the car that were for this purpose but they were too short. We found some long wooden boards that were holding down a cover on a garden in the field. Whit and Jack put them under the car in front of the back tires. They were able to squish them under the edge of the front part of each tire. Once we could get the tires up on those boards Connie would be able to gun the car and move it out of the soggy mud holes.

Jack and Whit got the boards all set and we again began rocking the car forward and backward to give it some momentum while Connie drove the car, rather gunned the engine and literally flew up and out of the mud hole and through the field. The boards had worked! Jack and Whit didn't get too muddy but my sneakers and legs were covered. Fortunately I had Bermuda shorts on so all I had to do was wash off when we got back to our motel. Another first and fun adventure!

* * *

The New Season Begins

What a great first day to open the camp… a clear blue sky, sunny, warm day, in the mid-70's. Whit and I arrived in the late afternoon after a breakfast meeting and visit with his old friends, Jean and John Makar in Somers, Connecticut. We had a lovely drive north through Massachusetts up I91 and across Vermont on state highway #103 and north on route #7.

The water pump had been turned on for the camps in our little cedar wood so we were able to connect ours, get the electricity turned on and everything else up and running.

We took a walk down to Long point meeting our friend, Mary Gordon on the way. She walked along with us out to the point and back. We chatted and updated each other on our lives after the long winter months. Mary, her husband, Bob and her Mom, Adele spend the winter months in Florida.

Coming back by way of the paved road and near the tennis courts we spotted a red fox that did not seem in a hurry to run away. He ran up the road and through a wood. Then we spotted him again moving slowly, perhaps stalking a prey through the field, backtracking the way he had come. He didn't notice us at first but soon did, and scampered off back into the underbrush of the woods. What a delight to see a fox so close! A welcoming sight for the beginning of the new season!

* * *

Church Friends

Sunday morning I was the liturgist at the United Methodist church in 'the hollow.' It was such a joy to see our Vermont friends there. Mari the minister was away but Marsha Hoffman, a woman from the Center Church, Ferrisburgh, gave a very fine sermon. She preached on how we are given tools to help God direct our lives. She shared the scripture from Psalm 105 the first five verses as a reference for daily living.

1. "O give thanks to the Lord, call
   on his name.
   Make known his deed among
   the peoples.
2. Sing to him, sing praises to him;
   tell of all his wonderful works.
3. Glory in his holy name;
   let the hearts of those who
   seek the Lord, rejoice.
4. Seek the Lord and his strength;
   seek his presence continually.
5. Remember the wonderful works
   he has done,
   his miracles, and the
   judgments he uttered..."

Psalm 105: 1-5, *The Holy Bible containing the Old and New Testaments with the Aprocryphal/Deuterocanonical Books*, New Revised Standard Version, Nashville: Thomas Nelson Publishers, 1990.

* * *

In the afternoon Whit and I enjoyed a canoe ride around our little bay and we took with us the mooring for the Boston Whaler and put it in. The Boat would be delivered on May 18th.

We walked again with Mary and visited her husband, Bob and her Mom, Adele, for a bit.

We drove to South Burlington to have dinner at UNO'S Chicago Bar and Grill. We checked out the movie theatre just up the road but did not find any movie that interested us.

* * *

A Peaceful Time with Nature

Monday we got up early, had coffee, and went out in the canoe again. What a joy to be out on the lake! No one else was out on the lake and in fact no one seemed to be up. The lake was calm, nearly flat, like a glass mirror. We enjoyed a peaceful time with nature. We saw a blue heron and several ducks.

* * *

New Mountain Bike

Whit went back home to Connecticut Tuesday morning. When he left I rode with him to Greenbush Road and walked back to camp.

I took a cup of coffee out on the deck, sat, picked one of the runes and read the meaning for it to use as a meditation for the week.

While sitting there I thought to myself, I have a new mountain bike. My daughter, Torrey had given me the bike for Christmas knowing I had wanted one for use in Vermont. So I put on the new bike helmet I had purchased, took my new mountain bike and went on a long invigorating ride. This was the first of many bike rides during the summer.

* * *

Barbera Arrives

In the evening my sister, Barbara, arrived from California. I picked her up at the Burlington International Airport.

Barbara would stay a month during which time we had some new memorable adventures.

Of course we walked our three miles each day as we had previous summers either to Greenbush Road and back or down to Long Point and back.

* * *

On Thursday, May 10th Barbara and I sat out on the deck watching birds in our cedar wood. We saw a pair of Baltimore orioles that seemed to be nesting near by, though we couldn't see the nest. A pair of robins were nesting in the under eves of the Gabrial cottage *Sunset*.

We saw blue jays, several sparrows, a couple of thrush, and two types of woodpeckers we couldn't name.

Later in the day when we did an evening walk around Long Point we were fortunate to see a mother Merganser and her babies, several of which were on her back. Quite a sight!

* * *

Birdbath Delight

It has been very dry and on Friday it rained.

What a delight! Several birds came right to the little angel birdbath in the front of the camp. A pair of cardinals, a robin, a chipmunk and a strange yellow bird all came to visit the little rock garden and birdbath. They were grubbing for worms, bathing, etc. None of them seem to mind the others.

The yellow bird we decided looked like a warbler of some sort. It had unusual markings of black, white, and yellow. Yellow lines that looked like glasses and a bright yellow belly. We stood and watched it from the screened-in porch, after the other birds left, as it moved up and down the path picking at the ground. I could have opened the screened door and touched it. It looked up at us but didn't seem to mind us watching.

Later in the month I described the bird to Pat Stacey and after looking at pictures in her bird book I decided that this little yellow bird might have been a yellow grosbeak.

* * *

Journey To Maine

What a glorious day! On Monday May 14th, Barbara and I got up at 5 a.m., this was first light, dressed, drank our special tea, packed the car and began a journey to the Maine coast. Barbara had never set foot in Maine so I had promised her I would drive us over for a day or two.

The day turned out to be a wonderful Vermont/Maine adventure.

We mapped out the route we would take on Sunday afternoon, and I admit we had some disagreement about this. However, our sibling stubbornness got straightened out and we made a navigational plan.

Our route was to take Vermont state highway #7 south to Middlebury, east across route #125 through East Middlebury, up through Ripton and the Bread

Loaf Campus of Middlebury College, and on past the turn off to Texas Falls in Hancock. Our first delight of the day occurred just past Ripton, Vermont on route #125.

We saw a moose sign. I commented that I had never seen a moose up close. (I saw one from a distance from a train when Whit and I had taken a fall excursion in North Conway, New Hampshire several years ago.)

I had just uttered those words when we spotted a young buck, a young adult male moose, standing on the edge of the road in some low brush and a stand of trees. He didn't move he just looked at us and then moved slowly into the growth.

We were stunned. What beautiful, liquid, round eyes! We couldn't say anything for the next half hour as we drove on toward Hancock and Route #100. And then we only had exclamations of incredible amazement of our sighting.

We drove south down Route #100 to #107 and northeast to Bethel, Vermont. We got on Interstate 89 and headed east across the Connecticut River into New Hampshire. It was a most beautiful, sunny, but chilly day.

We stopped in Epson, New Hampshire to fill the gas tank about 9 a.m. and to have a coffee and coffee roll. We spent about a half hour there, including two stops, looking for a special battery for Barbara's camera.

Driving on across to Concord, New Hampshire we headed north on Interstate 93 for about five miles and then east again on New Hampshire Route #4 to Portsmouth.

We couldn't decide if we wanted to get onto Route #1 heading north or Interstate 95 so we drove into Portsmouth and around in a big circle before getting onto I95 and heading northeast into Maine.

We got off at York driving through this quaint little village on Route #1A. There was a lot of work being done on the road, but we persevered and found a local beach where we could park, get out and view the ocean.

There was a walkway going along the beach and cliffs so we took a short walk. Barbara took pictures of her first view of the Atlantic Ocean in Maine. We then drove along this lovely coastal highway through Wells, and Ogunquit. We stopped at several scenic spots along the coast.

We stopped at the Nubble Lighthouse at York Beach, walked around, took pictures and received pleasure in the marvelous view of the very dark blue turbulent ocean and nearby high cliffs. There were little benches in memory of people who either lived in the area or had vacationed there.

We continued on our way and stopped at Perkins Cove, part of Ogunquit, Maine. We walked the area that had many tourist shops and restaurants. We looked for Barnacle Billy's, a restaurant that my friend Judy Gray had told us about. Barbara was not interested in eating seafood, meaning scallops, lobster, etc., so we ate lunch at the Hurricane Restaurant because it had fish as well as other types of meat fare.

I ordered a delicious meal of lobster chowder, a plate of mussels in a tomato, garlic, onion sauce and coffee to drink. Barbara had a swordfish stuffed with Brie, vegetables with an apple slaw and carrots with zucchini. Barbara had crème brule with blueberries and sliced strawberries. While enjoying this wonderful food we had a grand view of the ocean.

Following our scrumptious lunch we found another walking path along the ocean cliffs and walked for about twenty minutes before turning around. So far the day had been fantastic!

By this time it was close to 1:30 p.m. We had to make a decision about whether we would stay in Maine overnight or head back to Vermont. We decided to drive until 3 p.m. and then turn around and head back toward Vermont.

What we did was drive north and inland so that I could show Barbara the area of Maine that Whit and I had rented a camp with our two daughters nearly twenty years ago.

We headed through North Berwick and north to Hollis, Maine and on north on highway #114 to Lake Sebago and Long Lake. I showed Barbara the Nason Campground on Lake Sebago where my family had rented a small camp for a couple of years. We parked across the street and walked the beach shore of the lake.

At Long Lake I pointed out the Augustus Bove House, the Bed and Breakfast where Whit and I had stayed a couple of times.

We drove northwest to Fryeburg, Maine stopping at a small lake and lovely little park area called Kramer's Landing to rest. We sat and ate fruit and then Barbara, of course, had to take pictures.

We then turned west to New Hampshire. We headed back down Route #35 through Meredith, and along the north shore of Lake Winnepesaukee. This lake is very scenic and an active tourist area in the summer.

We drove across #104 to #4 to I89 and back the way we had come from Bethel.

As we drove over Vermont highway #125 past Ripton, Vermont we were incredibly awed again at the sight of a young male buck, moose. It had to be the same one. Awesome!

We had commented, "Wouldn't it be great to see the moose." And so God provided. There he was waiting in the same grove of trees. We drove slowly past him and then turned around and went back. He stood there watching us. As we turned around once more to head home he looked at us and slowly moved away. We could hardly believe our good fortune. We knew we had just had the 'icing on the cake', a double treat.

We arrived home at about 9 p.m. exhausted but having enjoyed an absolutely glorious and blessed day!

* * *

A Family Visit

My daughter, Torrey, arrived in the late evening from Connecticut the following Thursday.

On Friday morning 'the whaler', was delivered as promised and Barbara, Torrey and I went out for our first ride of the season.

Joy! Oh what joy! There is nothing more wonderful than being out on Lake Champlain!

* * *

The University of Vermont Bookstore is going to carry my first book, *Choices A Journey of Faith - Torrey's Miracle.* Barbara and I drove up to Burlington with Torrey in the afternoon so she could buy some items she wanted. UVM is her alma mater.

The book *Choices A Journey of Faith* ... is about Torrey, her healing and survival as a cancer victim. So when I asked the bookstore personnel about carrying the book they were more than happy to.

I also told them that this book had been revised and given a new title *Torrey's Miracle - A Matter of Choice* and that it would be out in the book market by mid-summer.

* * *

Friday evening Jenny, my niece, arrived from Boston.

Saturday morning Whit arrived from Connecticut.

The weekend was spent going on boat rides in 'the whaler,' *CHOICES,* playing hilarious games of cards, reading, eating and enjoying this wonderful spot on Lake Champlain!

While we were sharing time together we also had to deal with the knowledge we had received that Jenny's Mom, our sister, Jeanne, had been diagnosed with cancer.

We were not totally blown away because we knew from her comments that she had already made the decision to have the necessary surgery and then go to the IAT Centre in Freeport, Grand Bahama Island, Bahamas for the Immuno-Augmentative Therapy.

This is the same therapy that our daughter, Torrey had received for her cancer and our sister, Bobbie, had received as a patient in 1992. Both Torrey and Bobbie are alive and well today along with other friends who have chosen this easy, non-toxic therapy.

* * *

Garden Treat

Monday morning found Whit and I enjoying our first cup of morning coffee up in the loft. Then Barbara and I went for our walk, this time toward Greenbush Road.

We detoured at a farmhouse where there are beautiful gardens planted. I had walked by these gardens for four years and we both wanted to see them up close. So, we knocked on the door and asked to see them. The woman was very gracious and said to go ahead though she was about ready to leave for work.

We walked to the back of the property. The gardens had hundreds of tulips of many colors, almost gone by, daffodils, narcissus, and the beginnings of later spring flowers, such as marigolds, etc. Lilac bushes were abundant too. Indications of later spring and summer flowers were apparent.

We arrived back at camp and I made breakfast for the three of us.

We decided we would go out in the boat after I did some work on the computer. Then we would have lunch.

Well, our plan did not work out.

* * *

False Start

After I worked on the computer Whit and I went down to take the canoe and go over to the mooring for the boat. We got all settled and I went through the steps to get the motor started. The motor wouldn't start. I was sure I had done each step in this start-up process. I primed the motor two or three times. I went through the steps of the procedure once again. Nothing happened.

Whit and I went back to shore in the canoe and back up to the camp. We went ahead and ate lunch. I called Bob Gordon because I knew he would be able to help us. Whit and I took 'the Whaler' to Gordon's dock by paddling it from the mooring sight. Even though it was not very far, just across our little bay it was hard work since there was a breeze and the current was working against us.

Bob came down to the dock. He went through the starting procedure. The motor started. I knew immediately what my problem had been. I had not put the throttle in its correct position. I had known this at some level and just kept missing that piece of information when I was going through the steps. Bob enjoyed my embarrassment and the lesson I was learning.

Barbara, Whit and I got our ride, but not before I was humbled and learned once more that I need to be absolutely sure of what I am doing.

* * *

Drive into the Green Mountains

The mountains of Vermont are spectacular in all seasons and of course Camel's Hump in Green Mountain National forest is our favorite.

However the mountains north where Mountain Mansfield, the highest mountain in Vermont, is located have there own beauty.

We have on many occasions taken drives up into Stowe, Vermont and the Smuggler's Notch area.

On one of the not so bright sunny days while Barbara was visiting she and I decided to take a picnic lunch and take a drive north. We headed toward Charlotte, drove east to Hinesburg, on to Huntington and North to Richmond. We then went north through Jericho Center to Cambridge driving along the western border of the Green Mountain range and Mt Mansfield State Park.

This was the same route Whit and I had driven last October. Now the drive was a picture of a different sort: spring colors of various shades of green, brown and yellow, also quite wondrous from brief rain showers.

We stopped in Jericho Center at the Country store for some items. We learned that this store is the oldest continuous open country store in Vermont. It was a fascinating store to visit as it seemed to have any and everything a traveler might need.

We ran into a bit of rain as we drove on but we didn't mind. In fact it made our excursion more exciting. I think that the colors are more brilliant in nature when it is not so sunny.

Leaving Cambridge we headed west toward Fairfax. We stopped along side the fast moving Lamoille River, to eat our picnic lunch.

Barbara had made delicious sandwiches, prepared a fruit salad for us and supplied us with a drink mixture of lemonade and tea. The lemonade was made from California lemons out of her yard.

We sat and listened to the rushing sounds of the river and wind. We noted the fresh green color of the fields, trees and hills surrounding us.

After a half-hour of picnic enjoyment we went on through the town of Fairfax to Georgia and Georgia Plain bordering Lake Champlain. I wanted to show Barbara the Torrey Cemetery I had come across the previous season and the former house of Capt. Brown Torrey. It was fun to share this history with her.

We then drove over the causeway to South Hero meandering our way on some of the roads that run along side of the lake. The islands of South Hero, Grand Isle, and North Hero and further north have a different quality to their beauty. I guess it is because they have no mountains, but are surrounded by water and have mountain views on both sides.

Arriving home after dusk from our long day, we ate a light supper and sat in chairs on the screened-in porch of camp. We relaxed and felt rejuvenated by a refreshing rainstorm.

* * *

Barbara's last week was a rainy one, but we still got in several long rides in 'the whaler.'

We took a couple of pleasant drives down Route #7 to Middlebury and west to Bridport along Lake Street near Crown Point and through Panton.

* * *

Unity and Oneness

On Sunday, May 27th it was my delight to preach again at the United Methodist Church in 'the hollow'.

I cajoled Barbara and my friend, Mary Gordon, into having a fight, Stan and Carol Smith into having a marital quarrel and Sue DeVos jumping in to their quarrel during the sermon. My part was to step in and stop them.

The theme of the sermon was unity and oneness, 'That We All May Be One'. It was fun to have these people act out what we are not supposed to do. The scriptures were from Revelation 22 and the Gospel of John, Chapter 17:20-26 from the Holy Bible.

I found out later that several persons thought the fights were real.

* * *

Drifting

Barbara and I went out in my boat *Choices* in the afternoon following our morning at church. We went for a short ride because it was questionable as to what the weather might be. When we got back I let Barbara off at the dock and went to the mooring.

My routine for putting the boat away is to catch the mooring, take the hook and attach it to the front of 'the whaler,' and attach the extra rope and hook on the front of the boat to the mooring. In this way the boat is doubly secured. I then put the motor up, tighten the gas tank top, take the key and put it around my neck. I then pull out the plug from the bottom of the boat for instant drainage and step into the canoe. I untie the canoe from the mooring and paddle to shore.

In this case when I had completed all the steps and gotten into the canoe I realized 'the whaler' was drifting away from me. My mind said, 'How can this be?' I knew I had hooked it securely. But what in actuality I had done was hook the boat hook to the boat and the rope with hook from the mooring to itself, so the boat was not attached at all.

I was able to catch 'the whaler' with my canoe paddle and get back in it. I had to put the engine down, put the plug back in, restart the engine and pull around to the mooring and again begin the process of tying up to the mooring and bedding 'the whaler' down until the next time. It was an important message once again to stay focused. I had to laugh at myself and I was glad that I had seen the boat drifting before I had paddled to shore.

* * *

Our friend, Lorna Brown, came to walk and have tea one morning and another day the three of us went out in the boat. It was a gray, chilly day but we went ahead. We had a great ride in spite of an overcast sky.

* * *

Spring Water

I had bought a porcelain crock for spring water and an oak stand at a tag sale in Connecticut before I had come to Vermont.

On Memorial Day our neighbors, Ron and Alice Gabriel brought us a full five-gallon water jug from the Vermont Heritage Water Company. I was really excited because I had tried to find a company that delivered to our area. And even though this company didn't deliver I knew where I could get spring water when I needed it.

* * *

Water of Life

"I am the water of life." This is Jesus' summation of himself in the scripture from Revelations 22 in the Old Testament of the Bible that I read at the Sunday morning service on the 27th.

I thought of that reading this morning, Wednesday, May 30th.

Barbara and I woke up to 45-degree temperatures and did our laundry. Through the morning it sprinkled off and on and in between the sun would peek out from behind scattered clouds. The wind had come up and the water on the lake was looking rough and full of white caps. We hung out the wash because of the wind and the sun but every few minutes it would begin to sprinkle. Twice we began to take down the wash but in the end left it hanging up.

I thought of God's movement in our lives through water…water by rain, in the lake and various waterways, for drinking and washing, and for our laundry. Water the symbol of our baptism as Christians.

After hanging the laundry we drove to Charlotte to do our walk on the De Meter trail with our friend, Sue DeVos.

We came back to camp, ate breakfast and considered taking the laundry down since it had begun to sprinkle again. However, in a few minutes the sun came out again so we sat on the camp deck and read books. It was still very windy so we wore jackets. By the end of the day our laundry dried in spite of the sprinkles.

* * *

The Ethan Allen Spirit II

A nice tourist attraction and fun ride to take out on the lake is the hour and a half cruise offered by the Ethan Allen Spirit II. It goes out from the waterfront in Burlington. Barbara and I took this cruise because we wanted to hear the historic talk that is given about this area of the lake.

One historic point shared that we had not known was that the breakwater along the waterfront in Burlington was built in the late 1800's.

The afternoon we went on the cruise there were some school classes from Bellow Falls, Vermont. The crew was getting ready for a wedding and reception that would happen following our trip. too. It was an absolutely gorgeous day for an excursion out on the lake as well as one for a wedding.

* * *

One of the very best times in my boat, *Choices* for Barbara occurred on the last Friday of her visit, June 1st. It was a lovely, sunny but chilly day. The lake was in movement but not too rough for going out in the little 'whaler.' We made a plan to go out for several hours.

Barbara made a picnic for us of salad, a bowl of cut-up fruit, and banana bread with a drink of fruit juice and tea. While she did this I went on an errand to the post office and to get water with my friend, Pat Stacey, who had returned to the Vermont that week.

Barbara and I packed our picnic, took books, the binoculars, and writing material and set out for a grand day on the lake about 1 p.m. We rode from our mooring in Pleasant Bay over just past the Kingsland Bay area. I cut the motor and let the boat drift. There were several fishermen in boats within our sight.

We ate our picnic, read our books, wrote in our journals and rejoiced in the marvelous panoramic view surrounding us. For nearly two hours we drifted. We were nearly to Thompson's point and Flat Rock when I started up the motor. We took a ride north up the 'broad' lake all the way to where the Charlotte ferry crosses over to Essex, New York. Turning around we came back to our bay by Long Point, went around the Dean's Islands, back to Kingsland Bay and back again to Pleasant Bay. A grand excursion!

* * *

More Car Trouble

On Saturday, June 2nd, Whit was supposed to arrive for the week but called to say that his car had had some difficulty. We didn't know when he would get here since the garage for his old Peugeot was not open on Saturday.

Barbara and I spent the day playing cards and reading our books since it was rainy and cold. We played the card game, Canasta, nearly everyday... usually one game each day that took just about an hour, while she was staying with me. We kept track of who won. On that day she was one game ahead of me: ten to nine.

* * *

Pentecost - The Church's Birthday

The church service to celebrate Pentecost, the church's birthday, was very festive at United Methodist. The sanctuary was decorated with red balloons that hung above two large vases filled with white lilacs and petite red carnations. Every pew had a red flag at the center aisle and those of us that sang in the choir and/or walked in the procession carried either a red flag or a straw with red ribbons.

For the children's time Pastor Mari talked about how the Holy Spirit descended upon the disciples and spoke about the church's symbol for it, a dove.

Jo Ann and Walter Simendinger from Gardiner's Island had brought their white cockatoo and Mari worked the bird into her children's talk. A beautiful cake was brought in and every one sang 'Happy Birthday' to the church.

* * *

Barbara and I did not get a boat ride in either Saturday or Sunday because of the rainy weather.

* * *

Dinner Guests

Sunday evening we had our friends, Bob and Mary Gordon, for dinner. Barbara made a delicious Mexican dip consisting of layered refried beans, mashed avocadoes with lemon juice, sour cream, chopped tomatoes, and grated cheese.

We were all disappointed that Whit was not there to enjoy our friends company and savor the grilled steak that we served.

* * *

A Surprise Treat

The morning began with a bright sun, blue sky, and 60-degree temperatures. A plan to take a picnic and go out in the boat was made.

Sue, Mari, Barbara and I walked the three mile round trip to the end of Long Point. On the way just past the former Ball farmhouse Mari spotted something in the trees near the ledge on the left of the road.

We all looked and to our great delight we saw several small fox. These 'kits' saw us but were not frightened enough to hide. They were scampering and cavorting around under the trees. Then we saw what might have been 'mama' fox and the little ones disappeared. We walked on having relished in a wonderful treat!

Sue had never been down to the bottom of the hill at the end by *the Limit* or the L'Hommedieu camp, so we walked down and out to the end of the point. Barbara and I shared some stories of that area of the point from our childhood experience, including our favorite cedar tree, the one with the bent arm.

On the way back we looked for the foxes but Mark Eisenhower's dog had followed us back and I think if the foxes were around they soon disappeared.

* * *

One More Boat Excursion

Barbara and I packed a lunch of fruit salad, banana bread and butter, leftover Mexican dip and crackers and a tea /fruit juice mixture.

I went out to the boat and prepared it for a long boat excursion. I added two gallons of gas to the six-gallon tank as well as taking an extra two-gallon tank. I picked up Barbara who had our packed picnic lunch and other paraphernalia.

We went for a long ride first, heading north all the way to Sloop Island and beyond. We came back down the center of the 'broad' lake and stayed close to the New York shore all the way past Diamond Island. By the time we headed in toward the Vermont shore near Basin Harbor and come back around to Kingsland Bay the sky had become overcast and dark clouds were moving toward us from the south and New York side.

Instead of stopping completely and drifting as we did on the previous Friday I slowed down to a trolling speed and we went along the shore of Kingsland Bay into Hawkins Bay around Gardiner's Island, across to Long Point, on around the Dean's Islands and back to our little Pleasant Bay. While going along we ate our picnic and felt the excitement of the beginnings of the weather change.

The rain did not begin until I had let Barbara off at the dock and had gotten 'the whaler' tied up to the mooring.

It was another invigorating time on the lake!

* * *

Monday afternoon Whit arrived after he had gotten his car repaired early that morning in Connecticut. The three of us took the ferry from Charlotte and went to The Old Dock House Restaurant in Essex, New York for dinner. This has become one of our favorite summer excursions.

* * *

Barbara's Departure

Tuesday Barbara prepared herself for her flight to go home. We all went out for the last boat ride that was grand in spite of an overcast day. Whit and I drove her to the Burlington International Airport for an early evening flight.

Following her departure Whit and I went to see the movie *Pearl Harbor*. Barbara and I had already gone to see it, but I didn't tell Whit until afterward. I knew he wanted to see it and I thought it well done, so I didn't mind going again. And I didn't want to be sad because my sister had gone. She had been here four whole weeks and they had simply flown by.

* * *

Whit and I got in three more rides in the whaler' before he went home on Friday. And on one of our walks we saw the 'Mama' Fox again.

* * *

Free Fishing Day

Saturday, June 9th was 'free' fishing day in Vermont, so my friend, Pat Stacey, and I took our poles and went out in 'the whaler' to fish. We spent three glorious hours on the lake moving from one spot to another casting our lines in. We didn't catch anything but had fun pretending we knew what we were doing.

On the way home we decided to motor over to a little isolated beach and find driftwood pieces. I found some uniquely shaped rocks for the rock garden and Pat found good pieces of driftwood. We loaded the boat up and headed home.

* * *

Gospel Festival

We made plans to go to the Burlington Discover Jazz Festival the next day, for its final day, a day of Gospel Music featuring Francine Reed, the Burlington Ecumenical Gospel Choir and local gospel singer, Tammy Fletcher.

The Gospel Music at Burlington Waterfront Park was great! A long day but well worth the effort. I have sung in a Gospel Choir for a short period in Connecticut and find the excitement and emotion of this music faith provoking.

This Festival in its 18th year was just one of many wonderful events that happens in Vermont each summer.

* * *

Fascinating Friends

On a weekend in June my two friends, Barbara and Marge came to visit from Guilford, Connecticut. They arrived early in the evening on Saturday, in time for dinner. I had the grill ready to cook.

After they got settled we sat on the deck drinking wine while I grilled steaks and vegetables for dinner. We relaxed and caught up on the goings on of home in Connecticut.

Barbara is my hairdresser at home and while she was here she cut my hair.

On Sunday they went to church with me and then in the afternoon I gave them a two-hour ride in 'the whaler'. We took the ferry to Essex, New York where we had dinner.

The weather had been rainy in the morning but by afternoon and the rest of the day it was an absolutely beautiful day. A perfect day for being out on the water of Lake Champlain!

* * *

Famous Dad

I knew that Marge grew up in Burlington and was actually in the same class with my friend Lorna's sister, Malia. What I did not know was that her Dad, Samuel Hatfield, a friend of Lorna's dad, was well known for his photography. He was very active in the SAR (Sons of the American Revolution) and the Vermont Historic Society.

Many of his photographs of historic homes and particular areas of Vermont can be seen at the University of Vermont.

* * *

Deck Washed

On a hot, sunny day, Frank and Vicky Loven came to clean the deck of 'Camp Lottie'. They are a young couple in our church and Frank had started his own business. I enjoyed listening to this young couple talk to each other through the morning. The little comments that married couples make to each other can be sweet and the little endearments, "Honey," "Dear," "Babe" are fun to hear.

When they returned on another day to put the new deck paint on I enjoyed them again. At some point I commented through the window, "Looks nice." The response from Frank was "Thanks, Babe." Vicky immediately commented that it was not her that had responded. I said, "That's all right. I'm not his Babe but I am someone's Babe." We had a laugh together.

* * *

A Dead Fox

This morning Pat came by to go shopping in Vergennes. She said, "I just saw a fox that has been hit on Long Point Road." She and I went back to the spot, found the fox and took it away to be buried. We thought it might have been the mother fox of the little 'kits' several of us had seen earlier in the month.

Later we took a ride in 'the Whaler' and had a very turbulent ride when the wind came up unexpectedly. We were on the New York side near Spilt Rock and had to come across the 'broad' lake to Thompson's Point and on across the Long Point. I was more excited than afraid, but was glad to make it safely back.

* * *

June 25th

Driving up the dirt road from Jonesville, Mary Gordon, her Mom, Adele and I listened to 'Climb Every Mountain' on a tape. On this sunny, warm day we were on our way to her Mom's former summer cabin up on the side of Camel's Hump. We drove along side the Winooski River and then along a mountain stream. Mary pointed out the places she and her children used to swim in the cold pools and the places where her Mom would leave her grandchildren with rafts upstream and then go down and meet them with the car.

Adele, a fascinating 90 year old, Austrian born woman, was vibrant with excitement as Mary was and I for them. We arrived at the former cabin and the young woman who lived there let us walk around the property; look in the house that although refurbished, was generally the same.

Adele was so pleased and kept remarking how delighted she was to be there. "We are back on our mountain!" she kept exclaiming. I knew the feeling. It is that one of joy, incredible blessedness at returning to a place of marvelous memories and it is the one I have every time I return to Vermont!

We drove on further up the mountain to a parking area for the Monroe trail that goes up to the summit of Camel's Hump. Adele had climbed this mountain hundreds of times in the twenty years she lived on the mountain until she was 70. She would walk out her back door, through the woods to find an old lumber trail, and on up the mountain along the Long Trail.

We parked, found a cool spot in the trees near a spring and Mary set up a chair for her Mom. We brought out our picnic things from the car and ate our lunch of tuna/egg salad, whole-wheat croissants, fruit salad, with juice and coffee to drink. Mary and I sat on a blanket and Adele in the chair. We spoke of this mountain that had meant so much to each of us. We lit a candle in thanksgiving for our grand excursion thus far.

While Adele sat and relished in the peacefulness of the woods on the mountain, Mary and I walked up the trail for fifteen minutes and back. I had never been up this trail so it was another new wondrous experience for me. My family had always climbed the mountain from the Burrows Trail above Huntington Station. Mary and I promised each other that we would climb the mountain again this season, perhaps in September.

Leaving this area we saw a ranger station called the 'couching lion' station. We stopped for a few moments to walk back down a trail to see the little pet cemetery that was there. The young man at the ranger station told me how Samuel De Champlain had called the mountain the couching lion... a lion lying down.

I had always known the mountain as Camel's Hump until recent years when someone had told me that old Vermonters call it the 'crouching lion.' This was incorrect and I was glad to know the real name of 'couching lion.'

We drove slowly down the mountain. Passing one of the places where there was a deep pool. Mary stopped and parked. Again while her Mom sat and waited in the car, sitting in this quiet, peaceful atmosphere, Mary and I went down to the stream took off our shoes and waded in the cold waters of the fast running mountain stream. We picked up flat rocks and skipped them across the water silently reveling in the beauty of nature.

Once again with the 'Sound of Music' as background we drove down through Jonesville, each of us in silence with our own memories of the Green Mountains of Vermont. A glorious God enhanced day!

* * *

Kayaking

I came home tired but revitalized. Mary asked me to dinner but I declined. It had been a day of rejoicing and reminiscing.

I thought I want to go out in the boat. I called my friend, Pat. She suggested I come there and go out with her in the kayaks. I had never been in a kayak, so I said, "I will."

An already glorious day was given the 'icing on the cake.' I learned quickly how to enter the kayak, paddle with a two-ended paddle and move forward into the lake. We spent two hours on fairly calm waters enjoying a different peacefulness, seeing a blue heron, merganser mother duck and babies, watching an air balloon go over the distant mountains. Awesome!

* * *

A Daughter's Visit

Jessica, her husband, Dan and Whit arrived for a four-day weekend. We enjoyed the boat even though it rained. I showed Dan how to run the motor. Jessica and I had fun while watching him drive standing up.

During a rainstorm on one of those days, the four of us had a rousing game of Canasta. Quigley, their Corgi had come too and he sat near us while we played cards.

* * *

Pre-Wedding Reception

Pastor Mari and Andy Clark's son, Ben, were married on July 7th. Mari and Andy invited the entire congregation of United Methodist and Centre Church to a pre-reception on July 1st at the church. This was quite a celebration. Following the morning worship everyone was invited to a brunch prepared by two woman friends of the Clarks from Burlington.

This delicious repast included a variety dishes: platters of cut-up fruit, vegetables with dips, small bite-size quiche, scrambled eggs, etc. The congratulatory fellowship extended to the pre-newly weds Ben and Rebecca by the people was a joy to watch and be a part.

* * *

Disappointment—And a Spectacular Evening

Whit and I were to go on the Fireworks Train to Burlington for the Fireworks Display as we had two years ago on July 3rd. However, his sixteen year-old Peugeot had been giving him trouble so he was unable to come. I told him when he called. "Don't come back until you have a new car."

I took my friend Diane and we went with Lorna and Mike from the Charlotte Station. This was another absolutely spectacular evening.

* * *

The Return of the Husband and a New Car

The following week Whit arrived in a Subaru Outback. I was so pleased that he had gotten a new car. Now I wouldn't have to worry about him driving here from Connecticut and breaking down.

We spent eight marvelous days together. No matter what else we did, everyday we went out on the lake either in the canoe or in 'the whaler'.

One of the days we took the canoe up into what we thought was Jim McDurfee's Creek also known on the navigation chart as Thorpe's Creek off Thorpe's Point. We found out later that we had taken the wrong fork of the inlet and had gone instead up Kimball Brook. We paddled as far as we could up through the marshland, filled with white and yellow lily pads all in bloom, and into the woods.

A great blue heron brought us pleasure as he took off out of the marsh and flew across the water into the trees, as well as the appearance of a couple of kingfishers and red-winged blackbirds.

Two days later we did paddle into Jim McDurfee's Creek and had another one of nature's splendid adventures into the unknown.

* * *

Adam's Ferry Landing

We put together a picnic one afternoon and drove south through Vergennes to Panton, Vermont to the Adam's Ferry Landing. This lovely spot faces the lake and looks across to Westport, New York.

Sitting in our beach chairs on the shore of the lake we took in the view of the high, but old mountains of the Adirondacks, listened to the water lapping along side of us, read our books, and ate our lunch.

The Adams Ferry Cemetery near by holds graves for the Adams family of Vermont for many generations. I knew of this family in this area of the state because our friend from Guilford, Connecticut now deceased, Dr. Elisabeth Adams was of this family. Though she had grown up over in New York near Plattsburgh she had told me a number of stories of her visits to Vermont as a child in the early 1900's to see her cousins.

She once showed me a picture of herself at age ten standing at the bottom of the fire tower on Mt. Philo in Charlotte. I have a similar picture of myself at age ten standing in front of that same fire tower in 1953.

* * *

A Great Breakfast Place

Whit and I like to eat out, especially when we can find a good breakfast place. I had heard about a little place in Bristol called the Squirrel's Nest, recently changed to The 'Legendary' Nest. It is a family run, homey restaurant. While Whit was with me we decided to try it and on Saturday we drove to Bristol. I knew where the restaurant was located, as I had driven by on several occasions.

We were not disappointed. All the breads, muffins, pies etc. are homemade and delicious. The place was filled with the local patrons but also we could see that other people like ourselves had heard about the good food offered and the friendly people there. We ate a breakfast feast knowing we wouldn't want to eat again until supper.

* * *

An Afternoon Tea

My friend Doris Knowlton invited several ladies over for a lovely tea. Fourteen in all we gathered on the airy porch of her beautiful home to visit with Doris and to chat with each other. Some of us did not know each other but that was okay. We all had a common denominator, our friend Doris.

Doris's daughter, Sally was visiting for a week from New Hampshire. She helped Connie, Doris's caregiver and friend, Ann prepare a scrumptious feast which included a variety of dainty sandwiches, small stuffed cherry tomatoes, fresh strawberries with a sweet cream dip, dark chocolate brownies, and other assorted goodies.

The tea was served from Doris's beautiful silver tea set given to her many years ago by her husband Richard.

The ladies enjoyed the festivity of the day, the visiting with our delightful hostess, Doris and each other. The best part for me was watching this very special woman watch her friends having a good time.

Doris likes to tell jokes so she told several to her guests. They were what she called church jokes. Our gracious hostess gave each of us a gift of her warmhearted presence and lovely home.

* * *

Things To Come

Our daughter, Torrey will be visiting camp in the next few days with friends, and my friend, Helen, will be visiting at the end of the month.

I have purchased tickets for this year's Kingsland Bay concert during the July Mozart Festival series.

Whit's sister Jane and perhaps his Mom may come to visit in August.

My niece Jenny Jones will be back to visit as well and my sister Bobbie. And of course all of the family will be back.

* * *

The Adventure Continues

And what of tomorrow and these visits to come? What new wonders will they bring for family, my friends and me to relish in? Of course there will be more awesome rides and further exploration in 'the Whaler', and in the canoe on Lake Champlain; excursions up into the Green Mountains; visits to new marvelous places yet unknown to us; wonderful and extraordinary unforeseen adventures that are bound to occur.

I don't know what comes next. What I do know is that for my family and me this grand Vermont experience will continue!

* * *

Figure 16 Torrey Morse and Aunt Barbara. Dan Hoey driving 'the Whaler'; Jessica Hoey and Quigley. Whitney and Margaret Morse out on the lake, 2001

PLACES I HAVE VISITED AND THERE IS SO MUCH MORE

Long Point, Lake Champlain
Basin Harbor
Shelburne Bay
Bartlett Bay
Mallets Bay State Park, Colchester
Otter Creek
Little Otter Creek
Lewis Creek
Mad River
New Haven River
Dead Creek Wildlife Management Area, Addison
Granville Gulf Reservation, Granville
South and North Hero
Grand Isle

Charlotte Ferry
Ferry from Burlington to Kent, NY
Ethan Allen Spirit II ferry cruise
Ticonderoga Ferry

Green Mountain National Forest including: The many trails within
Camel's Hump State Park, on Mt. Abraham, Mt. Ellen, Mt. Lincoln, and mountains of northern Vermont, Mt. Mansfield the highest mountain in the state.
Robert Frost Interpretive Trail, E. Middlebury, VT
Spirit in Nature walking trails, E. Middlebury, VT
Texas Falls Trail, Hancock, VT
DeMeter Trail, Charlotte, VT
Shelburne Bay Trail, Shelburne, VT
Burlington Bike Path and Walk Way

Kingsland Bay State Park, Ferrisburgh, VT
Rokeby Museum, Ferrisburgh, VT
Ferrisburgh Artisans Guild, Ferrisburgh, VT
Lake Champlain Maritime Museum, Ferrisburgh, VT
Button Bay State Park, Ferrisburgh, VT
Mt. Philo State Park, Charlotte, VT
Shelburne Museum, Shelburne, VT
Shelburne Farms, Shelburne, VT

Battery Park, Burlington, VT
The Waterfront, Burlington, VT
Sheldon Museum, Middlebury, VT
Birds of Vermont Museum
Quechee Falls, Quechee, VT
Elmore State Park
Lake Carmi State Park, Franklin, VT
Caspian Lake, Greensboro, VT
Lake Dunmore
Lake Willoughby
Adams Ferry Landing, Panton, VT
Bennington Battle Monument, Bennington, VT
Mt. Independence State Historic Site, Orwell, VT
Fort Ticonderoga, Ticonderoga, NY
DAR Museum, Addison, VT
Sheldon Museum, Middlebury, VT
Chimney Point State Historical Site, Addison, VT
Hubbardton Battlefield, East Hubbardton, VT
President Calvin Coolidge State Historic Site, Plymouth Notch, VT
President Chester A Arthur State Historic Site, Fairfield, VT

Proctor Quarry, Proctor, VT
Puppet Museum
Shoreham Covered Railroad Bridge, Shoreham, VT
Fisher Covered Railroad Bridge, Wolcott, VT
Ethan Allan Homestead, Burlington, VT
Robert Frost Homestead, Hancock, CT
The Round Church, Richmond, VT
Calais Church, East Calais, VT
Cabot Cheese Factory, Cabot, VT
Teddy Bear Factory, Shelburne, VT
The Old Brick Store, Charlotte, VT
Ben and Jerry's Ice Cream Factory, Waterbury, VT
Cabot Cheese factory
Country Store, Weston, VT
Country Store, Rockingham, VT
Kennedy Brothers, Vergennes, VT
Frog Hollow State Craft Centers, Middlebury, VT, Burlington, VT

University of Vermont
University of Vermont Library, Archives, Campus

Castleton State College, Castleton, VT
Norwich University, Norwich, VT
Middlebury College, Middlebury, VT
Vermont Law School, Royalton, VT
Bread Loaf Campus of Middlebury College, Ripton, VT

Vermont Opera House, Vergennes, VT
Numerous Cemeteries of Vermont
Many Covered Bridges
Numerous Restaurants

SUMMER EVENTS I HAVE PARTICIPATED

Vermont Mozart Festival Concerts
Vermont Symphony Concerts
Burlington Discover Jazz Festival
Vermont Antiques Dealers' Association Show, Manchester, VT
Balloon Festival, Essex Junction, VT
Fishing Derby in June
Numerous Church Fairs and Potluck Suppers
Champlain Valley Fair
Rutland Train from Bellows Falls to Chester, VT
Fireworks train Middlebury to Burlington, VT
Variety of Craft Fairs

ABOUT THE AUTHOR

Margaret Berger Morse, the daughter of a Presbyterian minister, lived in several states over a period of forty years. She says the one place where she and her three sisters had the most pleasure with their parents in a complete, stable, and undisrupted environment was when they vacationed each summer in a rented camp on the shores of Lake Champlain in North Ferrisburgh, Vermont. This book was written as a memoir of those happy times.

In *Vermont Life Stories* Mrs. Morse writes of the wonder and beauty of Vermont enjoyed during those long ago vacations on Lake Champlain and in the Green Mountains. She shares many fun-filled and joyous adventures experienced with her three sisters then and at recent reunions. She has shared life stories from the summer seasons with her husband, Whitney, daughters Torrey and Jessica, and families at their own Camp "Lottie." Mrs. Morse has given emphasis to the local population and the flavor these characters have brought into all these experiences.

In 1986 following an eighteen-year career in elementary education, Mrs. Morse changed roles and began a new career working within "the church" as an administrator, volunteer choir director, and lay preacher. Mrs. Morse retired from that vocation in 1997 and wrote her first book, *Choices: A Journey of Faith*, the story of her family's walk with cancer and the eventual healing of their daughter. A revision of that book was published in 2001 entitled *Torrey's Miracle—A Matter of Choice* by 1st Books Library.

Mrs. Morse holds a BS Degree in Elementary Education from the University of Hartford, an MS degree from Central Connecticut State University, and an MA in Theological Studies from Hartford Seminary.

She currently resides in Connecticut and Vermont with her husband, where she writes and gives spiritual direction. This author continues to seek and relish the awesome beauty of New England as a hiker/walker, swimmer, and boater on Lake Champlain.